Paperback   ISBN 978-1-7349715-0-7

This book was printed in the United States of America.

Contact Us:

T: 866-285-9224

Kasperavery @gmail.com

Printed in the United States of America

9 8 7 6 5 4 3 2 1 0

CONTENTS

Dedication

Beginning Thoughts

Confessions of Josie Harris

Thirty Years Earlier

Josie Harris' Own Words

In Memory of Josie Harris

Dedication

We would like to dedicate this book to all victims and survivors of domestic violence. Josie Harris' experience with domestic violence was real. She understood how one could become addicted to, used to, or blinded by mental and physical abuse, and she was not alone in this: Rihanna, Cardi B, Kim Kardashian West, Tyler Perry, and Nicki Minaj, just to name a few, have shared similar stories.

Sharing our stories and overcoming the fear of reporting an act of domestic violence is imperative to effect change. We must no longer remain silent, allowing our abusers to get away and leaving the door open for the next victim. Domestic abuse can happen to anyone; whether you're young or old, rich or poor—it truly doesn't discriminate. Overcoming domestic violence takes brave women; women who choose not to be victimized and who fight for their rights.

Please share Josie Harris' story to aid in reducing the problem that domestic violence has caused so many; you never know whose life you can save.

Beginning Thoughts

September 9, 2010

Excruciating, searing pain blasted through my head. A blinding flash of light penetrated my brain as I tried to open my eyes. I thought my head was exploding, and I heard myself scream; my body struggled out of a foggy sleep. I felt myself falling… no, I was being pulled off the sofa. Was this a terrible nightmare?

When I hit the floor, it jolted me into awareness of what was happening, and I looked up as I tried to gain some traction with my feet to fight off this nightmare. But it was no nightmare—it was a real predator. I was not surprised when I saw it was Floyd, nor when I realized he was trying to hurt me that night. It had happened before, but this time, it felt as though it would be my last day on earth. As I gained enough energy all I could do was scream "FLOYD NOOOOO!"

Confessions of Josie Harris

August 2011

My name is Josie Harris. I'm a 31-year-old African-American female. Today I am a single mother with three children: Koraun, Zion and Jirah Mayweather. On the journey of motherhood, I discovered the one love that we possess. I believe it is that love that will guide us throughout our lifetime.

I became a victim of domestic violence a long time ago and it continued for years. You may not know my name, but I'm sure you heard of my ex-boyfriend and father of my children, welterweight champion, Floyd Mayweather Jr. I met when I was 16 years old, he was 19. From the very beginning we lived each day supporting each other emotionally and mentally, yet unbeknownst to us, the relationship would later spiral into something dysfunctional for both ourselves our kids.

I write this book to share my story; especially after triggered by numerous—usually incorrect—"facts" and rumors that have been reported in the press. These press stories were told by people who had no insight into our relationship. Being a celebrity means being in the spotlight, so there will always be people who think they know your story, your truth. It's my time to tell my truth.

You may ask yourself, "Why is she writing this book?" I needed to write this book to shed light on abusive relationships. No, I'm not an embittered ex; I still have love for Floyd. No, I'm not writing this with the hope of getting him to love me again. That kind of love is gone.

Now, let me take you back to the beginning.

Thirty Years Earlier

Where's My Daddy?

I was not fortunate enough to have my birth father in my life. At an early age I knew what emptiness and loneliness felt like. Many of my friends were raised by both parents, and I witnessed what balance looked like through their lives. When a young girl grows up without her father—or a father figure—in her household, it leaves a gap in he life, a gap that she tries to fill by looking in all the wrong places. Typically, the father is the first male figure to tell a little girl he loves her. A real father does not only say he loves you, but he also shows it. He should demonstrate how a man should treat his daughter as she becomes a woman. When true love is known at an early age, a child grows up knowing what love looks and feels like. These days, a teenage boy or young man would tell a girl or woman he loves her simply to get her in the bedroom. When I used the word love in the past, I meant every word of it; I played for keeps, while boys and immature men played for fun.

I often wonder where would I be if my father were in my life to teach me the things I needed to know, especially when it came to love and dating. But, the fatherly love I lacked caused me to build up plenty of love to share with what I thought was the right man. Most black men aren't showing their sons how to love, respect, treasure, or treat a woman. Many are teaching their sons how to be strong and fearless, how to stay out of prison, and how to survive in this unfair world we live in. Some aren't teaching them anything at all.

A woman can never replace an absent fathers' love with a man's love. A man attempting to fill the role of a father for his woman will do one of two things: he will begin treating you as if you were his child—making you feel trapped like a slave to a master. Alternatively, he will never show you the respect and love you deserve, he will just say what he thinks you want to hear to get what he wants in the moment.

Many days and nights I would sit in the living room watching TV and I would stare at my mom. My mom would come home from work, grab a glass of wine, pull out a cigarette, and she would sip and puff. I would sometimes wonder what was going on in her mind. Was she missing my dad? Did my dad hurt her, causing her to fall into such sadness, or did she drink and smoke to relax after a hard day's work? I'm sure working two jobs would drive anyone to drink or smoke, especially while trying to raise children on your own. My mom was the only person I trusted while I was growing up. She always kept it real even though she knew at times it would hurt me; as a grown woman I appreciate her realness and wouldn't change it in any way.

At times I would daydream about my life and what my life would look like when I got older and had children. Would my kid's father leave us like my dad left? Would we be married and live life until death do us part? Would I become a single mom on welfare standing in line at the grocery store with an EBT card, while carrying bags of food on public transportation like many other women? Then I wondered: would I drink every day after work or smoke a pack of cigarettes by bedtime? Would I do what it took to make sure my children and I had a roof over our heads, food on the table and clean clothes? As a young girl I couldn't help but wonder about how my life would end up or who I would become. There were times I wanted to ask my mom about my father and her life, but I found myself staying silent because I could sense she was going through something and I didn't want to make it worse. I'm sure this was her way of suppressing her emotions to make it from one day to the next. I cannot judge her because she was a great mom and did what she had to do to survive. She taught me a lot in my early life.

Family Affair

After a good night's sleep I woke early Thursday morning and went downstairs to join the family for breakfast. My brother, Quincy, sat across from me; I looked across the table and all I could do was shake my head and roll my eyes. That Thursday morning was no different than any other Thursday morning. He was strung out and looked to be in pretty bad shape. He looked like shit: his body was emaciated and tired, his deep-brown eyes seemed dazed.

It was the first time I had seen my brother since he and his friends made a scene in front of our mother 2 days ago. When I got home the night before, my mom was passed out again at the kitchen table with an empty bottle of wine. My brother sat staring at the empty bottle and the overflowing cigarette butts in a nearby ashtray. He searched through the butts, looking for any part of a cigarette left to smoke.

I was angry at my brother! "When are you going to get off that stuff and stop drinking? You're too damn old to sit around and do nothing, Quincy.

You need to find a job and start trying to help mama. She's working 10 to 12 hours a day just to make ends meet while your lazy ass sits around doing nothing." Who would have thought that Quincy Harris would grow up to become a dope-head and an alcoholic? "You are a damn disgrace and you make me sick to my stomach. Believe it or not, mama worries about you all the time, and the next time you steal money from her I will personally give you a beat down." God said: A child that steals from his parent(s) is no more than a common theft. "If you don't want to quit doing drugs and drinking then find another way to support your habits. Stop acting stupid!" I yelled to Quincy.

"I got nothing in my life…I'm doin' the best I can," he answered as his smile disappeared into sadness. For a second, I felt sorry for my brother. Reality suddenly hit me all I could do was shake my head. "Josie, it's not easy for me!" Quincy yelled.

"Hah!" I answered. "Do you think it's easy for any of us? Mama is trying to make a better life for us. I get up at six o'clock every morning, get ready for school, then catch the bus to work and stay there for 8 hour shifts every chance I can. I babysit on the weekends for another 6 to 8 hours. Do you think that's easy? No! Yet, you never hear me complain." I paused and waited for his response. He was silent. "That's how we're able to eat. It's the only way I know how to help mama. I don't ask her for money. You're a grown ass man and all you do is bring your friends here and eat up all the food. Who do you think pays for that?" I shouted. I got up from the kitchen table and walked over to the refrigerator and swung open the door. "Look at this, Quincy! We got no groceries and it's another week before mama get paid. What are we going do? Think about that!"

"I work when I can. There's nobody who will hire me." Quincy said with his head down.

"Why would they? If you walked into my establishment, I wouldn't hire you either. You look like an addict and walk like a thug with your pants hanging off your behind. There's something else you probably don't think I know! You're selling dope downtown. Of course that money never makes it back to this house!"

"Our father ought to be supporting us not you or me!" Quincy screamed out angrily.

I rolled my eyes and shook my head. "That's never going happen. His new woman, Linda, gets that money. When daddy left mama, he left us all for his new family."

My brother's hands were shaking as he picked up the glass of water that I placed in front of him earlier.

"Well without daddy, I might as well be dead!" Quincy screamed while placing the water back down on the table. That was a bunch of BS and a front for mama. All he cared about was that crack house and I am willing to bet if he could get his hands on a rock he would go missing again. Since our dad left, Quincy would stand outside of our house and look across the street at the house where my dad and his new girlfriend lived. Yeah, he moved in with the neighbor across the street. Knowing that my father left to be with another woman was bad enough, but the fact that he lived across the street really affected Quincy mentally. He could not understand. I was too young to remember anything about him; in fact I was just one year old when my father left. My brother blames that bitch Linda for breaking up our home and I agree with him.

12

As much as I wish I could use the word 'happy' to describe my upbringing, I'm not sure my home was all that happy. When I asked my mom about my dad's absence she said that he began an affair with the woman across the street. My mom was pregnant with me when he started seeing Linda. A few days after I was born he moved out of our home and moved in with Linda. A few months later he divorced my mom and married that bitch. He never paid child support like most men in America, so we struggled. Many years later I ran into my dad and he finally told me the reason he left my mother. He said she had a very bad gambling problem. The final straw for him was when he got a new credit card; he tried to use it to pay for a business luncheon and it was declined. He called to find out why, explaining to the company that it was his first time using the card. He found out that my mother had already maxed the credit card, the entire five thousand dollars was gone just like that! Every penny went to the Casino.

After hearing his side of the story I could no longer blame him for leaving; I would have done the same. At that moment, I said to myself, "I never want to depend on anyone to make ends meet." Everyone in my family had to look to someone to support them and I refused to get caught in that web. I was going to have more than a county- check and food stamps when I grew up. I tear up just thinking of our family struggles.

There wasn't much for me to say at that point. All this time I hated my dad for leaving my mother, when in fact it was my mother who left mentally when she chose gambling over her husband and family. In life we choose our own journey. We can't live another person's life for them; we only get to live our own. As much as it hurt me inside seeing my brother go through what he was going through, I realized I must be strong for our family. I chose to live before I die and I hope and pray that one day my brother chooses the same.

Absent But Not Forgotten

Teenage Years

After two years of my run-around boyfriend, Tony, I was finally
in agreement with my mom and what she always said to me: "He is
totally irresponsible and I needed to move on." I must admit, I was a
'hot ass' since I lost my virginity to Clint, my first boyfriend from the
neighborhood. All I could do was think of sex. I'm sure he saw it in my
eyes. At the age of 13, I thought I was in love, but really what I felt was
a deep connection with someone, a connection that I searched for in my
mother. With her working most of the time, she rarely had time for me. I
ended up hooking up with Tony right after Clint and he became the father
I never had. He was older than me, he was 16, but he acted older than his
age. Tony came into the picture when I was an irresponsible and reckless
teenage girl with no direction. I was only 14 years old and I'd already had
2 abortions; the first one my mom knew nothing about.

Neither Tony nor I were ready for kids—hell, we were kids ourselves.
The last thing I wanted was for my mother to find out that I was pregnant.
As much as I tried to keep it a secret, she ended up finding out and all
hell broke loose. I remember it like it was yesterday: it was the morning
of my appointment to have an abortion. After grabbing me by my hair
and talking to me like I had killed someone, she made an appointment
to see our family doctor. My mom might have killed me if she knew that

16

abortion wasn't my last. After the procedure, my mom made sure our doctor prescribed birth control pills for me to take. After that there was not a day that went by when she would not ask me, "Did you remember to take your pill Josie?" When I look back on my crazy life, I wish I had talked to someone before I chose to have sex. I was never taught that giving yourself away is something to cherish and remember forever; that you shouldn't give yourself to anyone just because you think they are cute or cool.

My First And Second Abortion

After the first abortion I remember sitting in my bedroom crying like a baby. I knew it was something that needed to be done yet it felt so wrong. I needed comfort and support but I was too young to be pregnant and didn't want the backlash from my family and friends. I always wanted to be a mother, but I realized I was too young to tackle school and motherhood, especially when the chance of becoming a single mom was high. When I decided to have a second abortion, I felt like I lost sympathy for life deep inside. What was I doing to myself and why didn't I learn my lesson the first time? Since then I have repented my sins to God because I know he knows I am not perfect and neither are my decisions. I also recall what the second doctor shared with me when I went back for my six- month check-up: "Young lady, you cannot continue on the path you're on. Every time you have an abortion you're doing harm to your body. The next time you decide to lay down with a young man make sure he has protection—not only to avoid being pregnant, but for your health mentally and physically. You also want to ensure you're taking precautions like birth control until you know you're ready. Sex without protection can cause lifetime disease, one that could have taken your life. Be careful."

That was the best advice anyone could have given me; advice I needed before this had all happened. After that, I didn't have another abortion, and when I did get pregnant, even though it wasn't planned I refused to go through what I went through earlier in my life.

Our First Encounter

It was the summer of 1996 when our eyes connected. I knew at that very moment and so did Floyd that this was no ordinary connection. When we first met, it was very casual—what most people would consider quite boring. We met at the local Bowling Alley in Las Vegas, Nevada. At that time there was a small community of blacks in Las Vegas, and this bowling alley was a place where kids of color who were under the legal age could hang out and have some fun. Although most of us were struggling teenagers, we have some fun times and formed great memories during this time.

Floyd was handsome and cool; he walked with confidence and a certain style. His presence was so overwhelming I could feel it through my entire body when he looked at me. I felt as though he had already made love to me before it actually happened. He had an attitude persona as he stood by the snack bar checking out the action on the lanes. The sound of the bowling pins exploded as the bowling balls were tossed down the lanes. The jukebox music created an atmosphere as he leaned against the wall. He looked at me with an intensifying glare as I came through the door to the snack bar. I could feel his gaze, so I played it cool and turned away, but

18

I could still feel the way he looked at me, it was penetrating. I would later find out that Floyd always got what he wanted, and on that night, what he wanted was me.

I turned around to look at him and he gave me a half-smile and nodded. He had so much attitudes, which secretly made me want to get to know him even more. The way he leaned against the wall as if he owned the world; he was like no one I had ever known. Was this connection a curse or a blessing? These questions would be answered and the truth revealed as our relationship unfolded.

"Hi," I said, feeling butterflies in my stomach, heart pounding. I was hot and bothered but I kept my cool. I didn't show any signs, we both knew the game, and we both played it. It was like karma: give a little, take a little. It was a romantic dance! We were both drawn to each other. At the same time, it was like a stand-off, and it definitely wasn't love at first sight. At the mere age of 16, my attraction for him ran through my mind and body. It was hard to stop thinking about him. My own private hope as a teenage girl was that our attraction would eventually grow into unconditional love.

He didn't move toward me as I stood at the counter, but his eyes and his smile were on me. I smiled back at him with my eyes and my body language. I acted as though I was flirting with other guys; like I could care less. It felt as if he could see right through my actions.

"Josie, right?" he said.

"How'd you know my name?" I asked.

In the background I could hear people joking and laughing. I could hear the sounds as the balls connected with the pins in the bowling alley.

Usually the activity in this place was dull and mechanical, but tonight it made me feel sexy. It felt like Floyd and I were the only two in the place; as if everyone else had been taken out of the picture, leaving only him and me in our own world.

Just then, Tony came up to me. Damn, I thought, he had ruined that moment. But it didn't bother Floyd—he just kept his eyes on me.

"I'm leavin' in a few minutes," Tony said to me as he turned and looked at Floyd. Floyd continued to stare at me.

"I have Mama's car, Tony. I don't need a ride," I said.

Tony had been my boyfriend for a while. In that moment I thought to myself: Wow, nobody has ever been able to get my attention from Tony. He was my world. At least until I crossed eyes with Floyd Mayweather. Floyd smiled and watched Tony shrug his shoulders and walk away.

"Is that your guy?" Floyd asked.

I shrugged my shoulders and thought to myself, "not anymore," but I kept my cool.

One of the girls who had been standing around the counter tried to get Floyd's attention. "Hey Floyd! Would you like to bowl?"

I started to laugh. He was way too cool for any of that action right now. What was she thinking? "Is that your girl?" I asked with a little sass.

He shrugged.

Floyd and I exchanged cell phone numbers that night before I left. I knew I would hear from him soon.

I was exhausted when I got home that night. I had been up since 6 o'clock that morning, had school until 3 o'clock., then rushed to my job at Goombah's Italian fast food. After I got off work I met my friends at the alley. It was close to midnight now, and all I wanted was to go to bed.

I walked into the kitchen and looked down at my Mom who had fallen asleep at the kitchen table. I was pulling the covers on my bed when my brother burst in the front door. I went to the living room and saw my brother and his friends. My mom stirred abruptly, she was trying to wake up.

"Shut up! Shut up!" I yelled at the three boys.

"Hey, wake mama up and let's all get high" my brother yelled.

He and his friends fell on the floor and rolled with laughter. Mom sat up and looked bleary-eyed at me and then looked at the boys.

"What time is it?" she said, trying to come out of the fog.

"Mama, I'm sorry they woke you. I know you have to get up early in the morning." I said.

My brother walked over to me, grabbed my arm and got in my face.

I glared back at him and before he had a chance to speak and yelled, "why don't you shut up and get out of here!" then I twisted out of his grasp.

When he lost his grip on me, he looked at me wild-eyed. I could see that he was high and there was no telling on what.

The next day when I woke my mom was already gone. I hurried to get dressed and rushed out of the door so I could get to school on time. Before I left home, I peeked in my brother's room but he wasn't back yet. I was sure he would return soon and I would continue pray for him each day that he would clean himself up and get off that stuff. I prayed that one day his conscious mind would speak to him and cause him to feel bad for his actions. All I could think was "How is this going to end for him?"

21

I was late for school again causing, me to run down the hall to my biology class. I slowly opened the door, trying not to bring attention to myself, and walked in. I took my seat across the lab table from a classmate, Bernice. Before I got settled in my seat, she whispered.

"I heard you met Floyd Mayweather last night?"

I looked at her for a short moment before I asked her. "How'd you know?".

"Vegas, it's a small town for gossip," she laughed. "I heard it from my boyfriend, he's Floyd's best friend."

"Yeah," I answered and smiled. "He's pretty cool."

"Well, yeah!" she answered quickly. "You know he's a boxer? Has been since he was a kid. I also heard that his dad and uncle were boxing champions back in the day."

"I don't care about any of them being boxers. All I know is he said he would call me."

"Is it okay with your mom if you date a 19-year-old? My mom would have a fit."

"She'd be glad if I dated anyone other than Tony," I laughed.

Bernice laughed out loud. "Right! Tony's just a handsome man-whore."

I shrugged. "He says he doesn't see anyone but me."

"Girl! You not really buyin' that bullshit?" Bernice looked at me. "Hell, you better go out with Floyd if he calls. He's ten times better than Tony and at least if he lies to you it'll be worth it. You know he has a girl, right?"

"I saw a girl hangin' out with him before we spoke. I think her name was Melissa."

Ms. Taylor, our biology teacher, walked over to our table and handed us our test papers and said, "I hate to interrupt your conversation, girls, but you are about to take a pop quiz and you have fifteen minutes to finish." I looked down at the test paper and I almost burst out laughing. It was a picture of a green frog on white paper with arrows, inviting us to identify its parts.

My purse was lying on the floor, but it was opened enough for the teacher to see my pager.

She paused for a moment and looked at me. "You know I don't like pagers in my class?"

"I know, ma'am," I answered, "it's not turned on."

Just as I reached down to zip up my purse, my pager started beeping loudly! Ms. Taylor looked at me and then she lifted the pager out of my purse and put it to her ear and pressed the button to end the noise that was now disrupting the class. Bernice and I turned and looked at one another in agreement—we both knew it was Floyd paging me. There had to be at least 4 shades of red embarrassment under my French Creole skin! Ms. Taylor put the pager back into my purse.

"You call whoever paged you back on your time, not the school time. Now you only have 13 minutes and I don't think this will be an ace Josie."

Bernice and I, along with the rest of the class who had listening to the conversation, started scribbling answers. We were all three minutes behind. Taylor was a be-achhh!

My boyfriend, Tony, was sitting across the room. I could feel his glare. I started thinking about how players like Tony don't want their girls to have any other dude, but think it's okay if he sleeps around with whoever he wants. I looked back at him and thought "Tony, it's a new day."

I was never a boy crazy kind of girl, but, when I did find a guy I liked, falling in love was easy for me. I would become totally dedicated to him; I'm what you call a one-man woman. I wouldn't see, talk, or go out with anyone else. My dude would become my world and my main focus. Of course at age 13 when I had my first boyfriend, I had no idea what love was. You can only guess what love is until you experience it. Just like many of the other young teenagers who think they've fallen in love, I thought I knew. After I met Floyd, I was sure there would never be another man I would ever love the way I loved him; so I gave him my heart, time, body, mind, and soul. Now I realize the only thing I loved was the idea of loving Floyd Mayweather.

"You all have two minutes left" said Ms. Taylor.

I looked up at the clock. Taking a test was the furthest thing on my mind that morning. I quickly scribbled my answers and handed it in. I was the last person in the classroom to leave. I couldn't wait to get home to see if it was Floyd who paged me. My girl Bernice and I went outside and met up. She was just as curious to know who paged me in the middle of class. As we started walking home she asked if I thought it was Floyd. I told her I didn't know because I didn't know his number. I did tell her I would let her know when I got home and returned the call to see who it was. We went our separate ways and finished walking home. As I reached the door, I pulled out my pager and returned the page. I ended up getting his voice message: "This is Floyd, leave me your name and number and I'll get back." He was a man of few words.

"Floyd, this is Josie, I'm sorry I returned your call late but I was in class when you paged. You have my number. Call me back."

Within a few minutes, my phone rang. It was him.

"Hello?" as I answered the phone.

"May I speak to Josie?" he asked.

"This is her. May I ask who is callin?" I replied.

"It's Floyd returning her call," he answered back.

"This is Josie," I answered while trying not to sound too excited.

"Did you ace the test?" he asked, laughing.

"I doubt it. All I could think about was that page and who it was."

"Where you gonna be on Friday night?" he asked in a sexy toned voice.

"I'll be at work until 9 on Friday."

"Where do you work?"

"Goombah. The fast food place in Green Valley."

"I'll be by 9:10 to pick you up"

"9:10 it is. See you then, bye," I agreed.

Oh, so I guess it was a date. I couldn't wait to hang up, scream, and call my friend and tell her all about it. I knew one thing for sure: I was ready for Friday.

Growing Pains

Meeting Pretty Boy Floyd

Our First Date

It was Friday night around 8:45 PM. I was serving my customers when I noticed a silver Jeep Cherokee pull up and park in front of Goombah's. A few customers were lingering around, while others placed their order. I looked through the restaurant's front window and a young man got out of the Jeep. It was Floyd; he walked up to the window and looked inside. As I took my customer orders I could not stop shaking, it felt like butterflies in my stomach. As soon as we made eye contact he started making faces and acting silly. I did all I could do to keep a straight face. I didn't want the customers to think I was laughing at them.

After the restaurant cleared, I looked back at the window and he was gone. I turned the other way and there he was, standing by the other window on one leg. I turned quickly so he wouldn't see that I was flustered and turning red at the thought of him disappearing. Then he walked into the restaurant, took a seat at the counter and picked up a menu.

"Hi Floyd," I said as I walked up to him.

"Hey Josie," he said as he sat wearing that million-dollar smile.

This man is fine as hell I thought to myself; I had to restrain myself from showing any real emotion.

"Give me a few minutes while I finish up. I need to make sure that everything is in order before I can leave."

"Can I order something to eat?" he asked

"We're closed. I thought we were going out to eat?"

"We are, we're eating here," he said as he smiled at me.

Floyd sat the menu down and walked outside.

"I'll be in the Jeep waiting for you."

I finished up and went outside where Floyd was parked. I walked toward the Jeep and noticed that he was not sitting inside. I stood on the sidewalk and looked around, then I walked over to the curb and looked down the street to see if I could find him. No Floyd. I began to get nervous. Suddenly, someone jumped from behind a nearby tree and scared the living shit out of me. It was Floyd. I slapped him across his back.

"You scared the living shit out of me boy." I said.

He laughed.

"Let's go," he said as he opened the passenger door.

"I see you're a real jokester."

Floyd got in the Jeep, started it up, and burned rubber as he skidded out of the parking lot like a crazy man. I suppose he was trying to impress me, but I wasn't impressed at all. I thought we were going to have a conversation, but he turned the music up to the highest volume. "Oh my God!" was all I could say to myself. A few minutes had gone by before he noticed my silence and turned the music down.

Floyd reached over and touched my arm and said: "Are you alright?"

"I'm fine."

"I can see that. Besides being fine are you cool?"

"I'm not into loud music, that's all. It's okay to listen to music, but listening to it at the highest volume is a bit much for me," I responded.

"I'm sorry. Let me turn it off."

He reached over and turned the music off and said, "I'm trying to make you happy, not sad."

"Thank you."

This man had no idea how many brownie points he earned for doing that one simple thing. When we got to the restaurant, Floyd pulled up to the valet and jumped out of the Jeep like he owned the place. The valet walked around to the passenger's side and opened my door. Floyd held my hand and the two of us walked into the restaurant. We walked in and waited to be seated. I was impressed. The man had a some class; this was a five-star restaurant. I felt like it was all a dream because everything was going a lot better than I ever could have imagined.

"How many?" the host asked.

"Two." He answered.

A tall handsome waiter escorted us to our table. It appeared that Floyd had made reservations and asked that we be seated in the back of the restaurant alone. I suppose he wanted some one-on-one time. The waiter pulled out the chair and waited until I was seated. We ordered something to drink and hors d'oeuvres. We had a lot to say to one another. He asked one hundred and one questions and I asked one hundred and ten. It seemed as though Floyd and I had a lot in common. He was quiet at first, but after about an hour his shyness disappeared. I made Floyd feel comfortable, at least that is what he said to me later that night. He opened up and began to talk about his troubled childhood. What took me by surprise was how intimate it felt when he started to share his story. Looking at him, I would never have guessed what he'd been through, so I suppose it's true: "You can't judge a book by its cover."

As for me, I was open at the beginning and I had a whole lot to say. Things I never talked about with anyone. Things that I stored away and tried to forget. I talked about the things my mother said to me when I was a little girl. I talked about the times I missed growing up without my dad around. Sometimes I felt as though I was the cause of my daddy leaving, because he left after I was born. "Why me?" I used to ask myself as a young girl. Of course he was not there to provide me with an answer. Anyway, one question turned into two, two turned into three, and so on and so on. By the end of the night I realized that both of us had a story to tell.

Our Shared Stories

"I hear you're a boxer?" I asked as I played with my food.

"I guess you can say that."

"How long have you been boxing?"

"I've been boxing since I was in the crib," Floyd answered and smiled.

"Yeah right!" I said while smirking back.

"I'm serious, my pops used to come into my room to change my diaper and I would punch him in the face. One time I hit him so hard I gave him a black eye."

"I think you missed your calling," I jokingly stated.

"What do you mean by, I missed my calling? He asked me in a real serious tone.

"You should have been a stand-up comedian instead of a boxer," I answered, laughing.

Floyd laughed so hard he spit out all of the food he had in his mouth onto the table. I jumped back, to keep from getting any of his food on my new dress.

"B-o-y!" Floyd wiped his mouth with the end of the tablecloth. "I'm sorry baby. I didn't mean to spit on you. That shit was funny as hell. Damn! You're the one who should be a stand-up comedian. I'm a natural born boxer baby girl. I'm the kind of boxer who will fight anybody."

As I pushed my chair closer, I noticed a scar on the top of Floyd's head. The scar looked like the letter "J." It was funny to me, because it reminded me of the first letter of my name, and I couldn't help but to ask how he got it.

"So Mr. Natural Born Boxer, since you claim you can fight so good, tell me, how did you get that scar? Did you meet your match in the ring one night, huh?"

"No, I got that scar when I was a little boy. I was in the second grade; I remember it like it was yesterday. I was running from this ugly girl who liked me and I tripped over my shoe lace. My head hit the fence and this scar is a reminder of that ugly girl chasing me every time I see or feel it."

I laughed; his sense of humor was which was one of the things that captured my heart.

"You don't believe me?" He asked.

"I believe you."

"I have been fighting ever since I could remember. I remember one week I counted 17 fights; some would say I was a bad kid but, everybody I saw wanted to fight ever since elementary school. I stayed in the principles' office and stayed on punishment."

"This is what I don't understand: If you kept getting in trouble at school and at home, why fight?" I asked.

"I don't know baby. I told you I was born to fight."

"Have you ever lost a fight?"

"When I was younger I think I lost one or two. That's because I started a fight with this tall ass dude. I mean this fool was bigger and taller than my pops."

"So, why would you start a fight with someone taller and bigger than you?" I asked.

"Because I was a big-ass bully when I was growing up."

"So, you just thought you could go around beating up on everybody?"

"Pretty much," he replied, shrugging his shoulders.

"Can I get you anything else?" the waiter asked us.

"No thank you." I answered.

"I'm good." Floyd answered.

The waiter sat the check down, "I'll take that when you're ready," he said.

"Thank you for dinner. I really had a nice time." I said.

"You're welcome and I had a damn good time with you. So, is this our first of many dates or our first and last date?"

"I'm gonna let you sit on that question for the rest of the night. So, are you ready?"

"Are you in a hurry?" he asked, his facial expressions changing.

"No, but I do have school in the morning." I said.

"I thought you were legal. Sixteen! Hell, I can go to prison for messing with you," he said, eyes bulging and voice trying to stay calm. "I'm good. No way am I going to get caught up and go to prison for some coochie. Hell no!" He reached into his front pocket for his money.

Floyd counted a total of one hundred and twenty-five dollars and laid it on the table.

He looked over at me and said, "Let's go baby."

I stood up, grabbed my sweater and purse and we left. It was a cold night and there was a full moon. We were standing outside waiting for the valet to bring his Jeep. I started to get cold. I thought to myself, Why would he say coochie? Is that all I am to him?

Floyd noticed I was shaking, so he took off his leather coat. He wrapped it around me and held me close to his warm body. I felt like I was a little girl in my father's arms. Of course I could only imagine what it would have felt like to be in the arms of my daddy, but this felt amazing. The parking attendant drove up with the Jeep. Floyd opened my door for me and made sure I got in safe before he closed the door. I fastened my seatbelt as he got in, and we drove out of the parking lot.

Just When I Thought the Date was Over

After driving around Vegas for approximately two and a half hours, we came to a stoplight on the Las Vegas strip. It seemed like every time we came to a stoplight, either Floyd or I would tell another story about ourselves.

"What does your father do for a living?" I asked.

"My old man used to be a boxer. Sometimes, I feel as though he wants me to become what he never became. My mother said I was around nine months old when my dad made me a pair of little boxing pads and taught me how to spar in the crib. When I got a little older he started imitating air punches. 'Left, right….right, left, left, right,' hell, those were probably the first words I knew how to pronounce. I had no idea what he was doing at the time, only my pops knew.

He always said to me, "You're going to be the next boxing champion of the world lil Floyd. Whatever it takes, I'm going to do it. By the time I teach you my unique fighting skills and quick reflexes, you will be one of the baddest motha fuckas in the world. Now you can take that to the bank.

"Even though I had no understanding about a damn thing he was saying then, my old man was no different than Michael Jackson's father Joe, according to what Michael said over and over. Joe beat the crap out of him until he got that shit right. They say practice makes perfect and fear turns men into bitches. A lot of the time I would catch my pops talking to himself," Floyd continued.

"Does your Dad train you now?" I asked.

"He was training me until he went to prison a couple of years ago; he's a son of a bitch and we don't always get along. My uncle, Roger is training me now."

"What did he go to prison for?" I asked, being nosey.

"Drug trafficking; he got busted like in 93. I'm in training camp right now. I am training for my next fight in October here in Vegas."

"Do you miss your Dad?" I was only asking because I was curious and thinking about my own Dad.

Floyd shrugged, "Like I said, he's a tough son of a bitch, but I can't take nothing from him. He was a bad motha fucka in the ring. Enough

34

about my dad, what about yours?" Floyd said, looking tired of answering questions.

"I'm sorry I got carried away with all the questions. The story of my dad is short because he left when I was one, started a new family, helped every now and then, and that was that. Did your dad raise you along with your mom? What I'm asking is: Was your dad around when you were growing up?" I was comparing our circumstances.

"He was around." Floyd answered as he kept his answer short.

"My Dad came around occasionally, but it always seemed strained when he did."

"Yeah, my pops was around, but for the first twelve years of my life he didn't think I was his son. My name was Floyd Sinclair until I was 12 years old. My mom told me he never wanted to sign the birth certificate so she gave me her last name. I'm sure it was his anger at my mom because she was on drugs, but her drug problem had nothing to do with my last name. I don't feel shit about my so-called father. All he ever did was beat the shit out of me when I was a kid."

"Did you do something to cause the beating?"

"No, I didn't have to do anything wrong for him to beat me. He thought I was his personal punching bag or something."

"Do you have any brothers and sisters?"

"I have two sisters. What about you?

"I have a brother and two sisters" I replied back thinking how we already had things in common.

"Do you think I'll cheat on you?" Floyd asked.

"I have no idea what you would do. I don't put anything past a man.

35

You guys have dog blood running through your veins. I saw my brother go through different women like a revolving door. Well, for your information, I'm a one-man woman. I don't cheat. When I'm in it, I'm in it and I play for keeps. I love fast, hard, and deep and I don't want to be hurt. If you can't respect that, I understand. Maybe I'm not the woman for you. The real question is would you ever cheat on me?" I asked, smirking.

"When I'm with a girl, it's me and her till the wheels fall off. I don't mess around. I believe what goes around will come back around and bite you in the ass. I ain't no dog home girl. I'm a good man. I'm the type of man that would get out there and work three jobs if I had to just to keep food on the table and a roof over our heads, especially if we had kids." Floyd responded as we strolled up and down the Strip.

By this time the sun was starting to rise and I found it hard to keep my eyes open.

"It's late boo. Don't you think you should be getting me back home now? I do have school."

"I'm taking you home now. I forgot that you had to go to school in the morning. I thought we could kick it all night long."

"We did."

"I'm talking, kick it, kick it."

"If you're talking about sexing me, wrong girl. I don't have sex on the first, second, or third date. I may fall in love easily but I never said it was easy to fuck me."

"I didn't mean it like that, come on. Look at me. Do I look like the type of guy that goes around having sex with all type of girls?" Floyd asked me, while smiling.

"Yes you do." I answered.

"You are different, but I like that. I see you're different than most other chicks in the hood."

"Can we change the subject?" I asked but by the time I looked up I was home.

"I guess I'll say good night or good morning. Will I hear from you tomorrow?" Floyd asked, smiling at the same time.

"I will call you later today Mr. Mayweather and you drive home safe," I answered as I searched for my house keys. I waved goodbye and he blew me a kiss.

All About My Man "Floyd"

In order to understand my life with Floyd, you would have to know a bit about him. Floyd was born and raised in Michigan. He had a rough time coping with life in the ghetto. Some nights his family barely had enough to eat. Other children were able to attend school, come home, do homework, go outside and play with the neighborhood kids, then come inside to eat dinner. Floyd had to train, run, and look at old boxing videos with his part-time father. Floyd and his family were poor. He was a very lonely kid he said he had a hard time building relationships with people outside of his mother and two sisters. He never let anyone close to him that he didn't know.

I learned more about his Dad, Mr. Mayweather Sr., and how he used to beat Floyd if he didn't want to train. Floyd was angry at times with his mom because she had chosen drugs over him and his sisters. It appeared that he had been left to fend for himself from birth. He was unable to make his own choices and he never got the love he needed and deserved from his mother or father. As they say, "What doesn't kill you will make you stronger." I can truly say today, in spite of what Floyd went through as a kid, it all paid off for him.

His father forced him to be something he didn't want to be and he became one of the best fighters in the world in his division. His mother was on drugs and neglected him, but that kept him away from drugs. Sometimes we feel like there's no one there for us, but God is always there. I understood and related to his pain and neglection from my own childhood; I too had someone in my family who was addicted to drugs. I knew what unconditional love was from watching the love my mom had for my unappreciative brother. She still loved him, even after he stole from her and lied to her numerous times. I wish I had that same love from my dad, but I didn't. The one thing I came to realize is you can't make anyone love you; they have to want to love you. One day I asked Floyd about love.

"Do you know what unconditional love is?" I asked.

"Unconditional love? That's like a dream," Floyd said as I laughed.

"As Tina Turner said, what's love got to do with it?" I responded.

Floyd never smoked, drank, or used drugs. I looked at him and my heart melted. Floyd had really been hurt and I started to wonder if he would ever get over it. I often wondered if he blamed himself for what his mother and father did in the past. I wondered if he would ever forgive his father for the negative impact he had on Floyd's life. Even though I was only 16 years old at the time, I knew that forgiving someone for their wrong doings would be a blessing to oneself.

As I listened to him, one thing I realized was how much Floyd learned to loved boxing. Even though his father made him train and fight when he was younger, Floyd was and still is a true athlete. He knew the importance of taking care of his body.

We both were silent for a moment, and then out of nowhere he shouted, "Boxing is my life!"

"Why boxing?" I asked.

"Because it's the one thing I can depend on."

I wanted to say to him that night that he could always depend on me, but I didn't think it was wise for me to expose my feelings for him so soon. I didn't want to let him know how much I cared about him and loved him, so I kept those thoughts to myself.

I hoped he would find the help he needed to overcome his hatred for his father, and that he would discover a true understanding of addiction. Addiction doesn't always mean drugs or alcohol. Addictions come in various forms, such as sex, working, shopping, gambling, cleaning, etc. A long look in the mirror could reveal an addiction barred inside ourselves. Find your addiction and you will find your true self.

Facing The Truth

After school I met with Floyd because I had something to tell him and I was hoping he wouldn't be angry at me.

"Hey babe, I have something to tell you and don't get mad." I said to him.

"What is it baby?" he asked.

"Your water pistols were confiscated at school today," I said, hoping he wouldn't be angry.

"How?" he asked, half-smiling.

I told him the story and he laughed hard.

"Hell, those security guards took them home to their kids!" I said. "I'm sorry, Floyd. We were just having fun. I had no idea they would take them away."

"You know what, Josie? As long as you had fun, that's what it's about. That's why I got them."

"We never had water guns and stuff back when we were kids, did we?"

I looked at him in awe. "No, we didn't."

"That's why I do what I do, Josie. I want you and me to have a better life."

"I love you, Floyd…" I said and put my arm around him and drew him closer to me. I could see my mamma looking at me. She knew I was in love and that I was hooked.

His uncle Roger looked a little worried though. It was clear to me that he wanted him to stay focused on his boxing, not on me and how serious we were becoming.

(**Love letter excerpt:** Dear Josie…I love you more than anything… Dear Floyd…Did you really mean it when you said that the person you love has to want to grow old with you so y'all can push each other in a wheelchair?)

Floyd and I wrote letters to one another throughout our relationship. My girlfriends thought our letters were so romantic, but for me and Floyd it was a way of communication, a way to understand one another. It was our attempt at finding our way to the road of love and success!

Las Vegas Fashion Mall

Floyd came to house around one o'clock the next afternoon. It was cloudy in Vegas, which was unusual, because the sun shines almost 365 days a year.

"Let's go to the mall. I gotta' get some things," he said.

When I got in the car he pulled out a wad of cash from the proceeds of the fight and showed it to me. It was all one-hundred-dollar-bills bound in a rubber band.

"Get outta here!" I said to him. "How the hell did you get all that?"

"Payday, baby," he said, smiling. "I need some new clothes. I've got an interview next week with one of the sports guys from ESPN."

We wandered through several stores holding hands. Every now and then I would lean over and give him a kiss. He was always surprised when I kissed him in public—he had never been around anyone who showed their affection like I did. He thought it was crazy, but at the same time he loved it.

We window-shopped for a while and Floyd scrutinized the new fads in men's clothing. He loved clothes and particularly, he enjoyed having brand names and trendy fashions. He always made a fashion statement, both in the ring and out. He saw some sweaters through one of the windows in the store that he really liked, and we went inside. Floyd was generous with himself and with those around him.

He kept asking me: "What do you want Josie?"

I wasn't sure what to say because I didn't want him to spend his money on me.

"Floyd, you buy things for yourself. I don't need anything right now.

Enjoy your winnings."

"Josie, winning is all about giving to the people around you. It doesn't make much sense to win if you can't make other people happy," he responded.

I knew money was still a struggle for us right now and I knew he was generous with gifts for the people he loved. But, just being with him was all I wanted, so I kept repeating myself. I was fine and I had enough clothes to wear for work and school.

"But when I start having interviews about being the girl of the world champion boxer, then I'll let you buy me some clothes," I teased.

He laughed and squeezed my hand. "And I'll say it's all cuz' of you! I want you to start following me on my runs with the car," he turned to me and asked, "do you want to?"

"Seven miles? I'd rather follow you on my roller blades," I said.

"You sure you can keep up? I run like the wind, girl, you know that," he said, teasing.

"Are you running tonight?" I asked.

"Um---hmmm….Every night…" he answered.

As we were leaving the mall, he pointed to an outfit in the window at a fashion store for women.

"Just answer yes or no…Do you like that outfit in the window? And no bullshit, Miss Harris."

I glanced at the window. "It's nice. I like the color. But, you like that color too. It's the same as the sweater you bought."

"I said yes or no, Josie" He repeated looking at me.

"Yes," I said and smiled.

42

He nodded. "You stay here," he let go of my hand and walked into the store. I watched him while he spoke to one of the cashiers behind the counter. She peered around him and looked at me. About five minutes later he came out carrying packages.

"What did you get?" I asked.

"Something you gonna' love," he said, tauntingly.

"What is it?" I played with him knowing, in the back of my mind that he went into the store to buy the dress displayed in the window.

"You still seeing Tony?" he asked.

"Where did that come from, and when would I have time to see Tony?" I asked. "I spend any free time I have with you. I'm done with Tony."

He didn't look convinced. "You better be telling the truth."

"I am, Floyd. I'm a one-man woman! Of all people, you should know that by now."

"Who's your man?" he continued.

"You are! Ever since the night I met you at the bowling alley you've been my man, before you even thought to ask me," I said.

I hugged him and kissed him again, right in the middle of the mall.

He looked at me once more and then took my hand as we walked out the door.

"You're crazy, girl."

"About you," I said laughing.

When we got in the car he grabbed the package he bought from the last store. It was wrapped up like a gift and he handed it to me.

"Open it."

"Floyd, I don't want you to buy things for me. That money you earn is for you to enjoy."

"Josie," he said, still looking at me, "open it."

I opened the gift box and it was the outfit from the window, along with a purse and accessories. I knew the sales lady had chosen the bag, but it was a favorite designer of Floyd's.

"I don't know what to say. No one has ever treated me like this, Floyd."

I could feel the tears starting to come to my eyes. It was so strange to have someone buy something for me that was so expensive; and it wasn't just about the price, but he was thinking about me too. This felt good. How could I not fall in love with this man? Isn't that what we all want?

"Josie, I want to buy everything for you. I want us to have a life that neither of us has ever had before!"

"I love it and thank you. I mean it from the bottom of my heart. Do you know you're the first man that ever bought me anything? And that includes my own father. Let me take that back: He did buy me a pair of $7.00 shoes one birthday, but forgot the birthday card. Now, let's go get my roller blades," I said laughing.

Young In Love

Our Very First Time

That Special Moment

Before all of the broken promises, arguments, and fights, which led to broken trust, we shared some good times as a couple. We travelled, went to dinners, partied, and went shopping, just like lots of other couples in the beginning. We went to the movies, to concerts, and of course to fights, which always ended with after parties. Floyd exposed me to places and things that I probably would never have experienced otherwise, at least not at such a young age. Those times I spent with Floyd were a dream come true for me and I will treasure those memories for the rest of my life.

One night after dinner Floyd said, "Hey Josie, pack a suitcase and call your girlfriend Kenishia; ask her if she wants to go to Cali and hang out with us and my boy Shawn."

"Ok Baby, I'll call her.'

I was immediately full of excitement and ran upstairs to pack my suitcase. I called my girl Kenishia and I told her that Floyd had invited her to Cali to hang out with us. She was just as excited as I was. Boy, was I happy to be getting out of Las Vegas and going to California with my baby. I had heard it was a great place to visit and I was thrilled to be going with my man and my best friend.

Hell, I don't think I had three dollars to my name. We talked about looking for somewhere to sleep, but because of our lack of funds, choices were limited. Needless to say, we didn't stay in a five-star hotel or the Four Seasons in Beverly Hills.

Before we drove around looking for a motel, we stopped at I-Hop in Inglewood and had breakfast. Floyd ordered pancakes with strawberries and whip cream, with a side order of scrambled eggs and ham. Shawn ordered the same except he ordered bacon. My girl Kenishia ordered pancakes, with bananas, strawberries, blueberries, whip cream and a side order of oatmeal; and I had pancakes with whip cream only, egg whites, sausage and hash browns. We ate, talked, and acted like fools in the restaurant until daylight. One of the things I liked about Floyd was that he always told jokes and made fun of people. The bill was $31.98 but Floyd came up with a plan, which was to run out of the restaurant and not pay the bill. We all looked at one another, not knowing what to say.

"I was just kidding. I wanted to see if my baby was down with ah brotha," Floyd said as he winked at me.

Everyone laughed, we clowned around like kids, and then Floyd paid the bill. After leaving I-Hop we drove around looking for a motel. By now we were full and exhausted. We drove around for nearly an hour before we settled in at a motel near Figueroa and 70th Street. It was $25 a night. Floyd paid for a couple of nights, then we grabbed our luggage and headed to our room. We were too tired to un-pack—we dropped everything on the floor, and fell across the bed. We yawned, talked a bit, until we all fell asleep.

Later that day we all got together and went to lunch. We decided to drive through Hollywood. It was my first time there and I was excited.

47

We took a few quick pictures and ended up stopping to eat at a hole-in-the wall fast food cafe. We each ordered burgers, one large order of fries, and a large Coke that we were going to share. After messing around in Hollywood we drove to Venice Beach, and man did we have some fun! We stood around and watched people perform different acts. I had never in my life seen so many people just walking around; it seemed to me as though they were doing nothing. After hanging out at Venice Beach we stopped and ate at In–N-Out. Finally, we decided it was time to make our way back to the Motel. Floyd pulled into the parking lot at the Motel we were staying at around 2:00 AM. Shawn and my girl went to their room and Floyd and I headed to our room, number 116.

I remember that morning like it was yesterday. It was the first time I made love to a man that I had a real emotional connection with. I had already given my heart to Floyd; whether he knew it or not, and I had already surrendered my soul to him.

"I'm going to take a hot shower baby," Floyd said as he started undressing right in front of me, one piece of clothing at a time. He pulled his white t-shirt over his bald head and threw it on the chair that was \ nearby. Then he kicked off his tennis shoes and removed his socks and threw them on the floor. He unbuttoned his jeans and pulled them down slowly like he was trying to seduce me. It was working but I showed no emotion yet. Soon his jeans were down to his ankles and he stepped out of them, leaving them on the floor. He stood there with nothing on except his white boxer shorts. He turned to me, flexed his muscles', and smiled. All I could do was smile, biting my bottom lip. "Um um" was all I could say under my breath as he turned and walked into the bathroom. That man has one of the sexiest bodies I have ever seen. Not to mention he is the first man I have ever seen with an eight pack.

After a half hour or so, he walked out of the bathroom wrapped in a bath towel. He lay across the bed and started kissing me. I wrapped my arms around his neck and kissed him back passionately. My body was as hot as hot baby oil and I found it hard to control my thoughts. I then pushed him back off me saying:

"Wait! Let me catch my breath baby. I need to take a shower."

Floyd looked at me and smiled ,"Go take that shower baby and bring that hot body back to me."

I smiled as I climbed out of the bed and walked into the bathroom. I got undressed in the bathroom because I was still shy, especially since this was going to be our first time. I took a shower, brushed my teeth, removed my make-up, and shaved. I opened the bathroom door and walked back into the room, where Floyd was laying across the bed naked. "Oh my God!" was all I could say to myself as I walked over to him, my bath towel wrapped around my body as I climbed onto the bed and laid next to him. He turned, kissed me, and said, "I'm glad you're here with me. I really, really like you. I'm serious. I haven't told anybody that in a long, long time and that you gotta believe."

"I love you." I interrupted.

"Do you boo? Damn!" Floyd responded.

"It's true. I felt this way the first time I saw you at the bowling alley."

"I believe you boo," Floyd said as he slowly removed the bath towel from my body.

Considering that this was our first time, and I was feeling a little

49

shy, I reached for the blanket and wrapped my cold body with it. I was trying to keep warm.. After a few minutes of foreplay we started to make love; OMG was it good! His kissing and touching my overheated, wet body turned me on to the max! At that time I totally allowed myself to surrender to him. I melted into his arms and entered into his soul when he went inside of me. The slow moves, the motion of his body and my body together was magical.

I had no idea what being in heaven felt like, but that night felt like heaven to me. This feeling had my thoughts going wild. How does a person want to turn over their whole soul to someone? That was the question I asked myself. This was the first time I cried while making love. It didn't compare to the times I was intimate with others in the past—this felt like something from another planet. At that moment, I was ready to become Mrs. Mayweather. Without going into too much detail about the things we did together, I will just say that Mr. Floyd Mayweather Jr. rocked my world and tossed my salad over and over again that night.

It was a very long, emotional, and passionate night for the both of us. The love and feelings I had for him had built up inside of me and now that love was at a point of no return. After a long time of fun and pleasure we finally fell asleep. When we got up the next morning we headed back to Vegas.

Our "First Time" Reflections

I sat in the passenger seat on our way back to Vegas, as the music played and everyone was talking and laughing at one another's jokes. I began to reminisce on the previous night in that raggedy motel and I

50

asked myself: "Was it really all that?" Now that I'm no longer that little, innocent, naïve sixteen-year-old girl, did Floyd really rock my world? Did he really toss my salad? Or was it all in my teenage head? Did I make myself believe that he was heaven and all the clouds? When I really think back, it was as though he was my first. I had been with two other boyfriends before Floyd. When I compare him to the other men, well, there is no comparison when it comes to the bedroom. I thought 4 inches was long, but now, 4 inches is an insult. I am the type of person who gives credit where credit is due. Yes, Floyd had moves; he was able to last a long time in the bed because the man was a beast when it came to training and exercising, but a woman like me needs more than the motion in the ocean as they put it. Nice looks don't mean that he is a "Mr. Man Dingo" lady, really. I'm sure I probably broke a few hearts and crushed a few fantasies when it came to Mr. Mayweather. I'm sure Floyd thinks differently, but isn't he supposed to? Most men believe they are God's gift to women, in and out of the bedroom. Let me put it this way: not all men were blessed in that area. These are simply my thoughts as I sit back and think about my first time with the champion, Pretty Boy Floyd.

Back In Las Vegas

We left Los Angeles and arrived back in Vegas around 5:23 in the morning. Floyd dropped everyone off before he pulled up in front of his apartment.

"Hey Josie, take the car home and call me later when you wake up. It's almost 5:30, the time I usually run and train."

He kissed me as he reached for his bag with his training gear. I slid over to the driver side and headed home, barely keeping my eyes open. I pulled into the driveway of my mother's house, parked and grabbed my bags. I locked the door and made my way to the front door. I didn't want to wake anyone. I tippie toe'd to my bedroom, opened my bedroom door softly. I made it! I dropped my bags on the floor, jumped straight in the bed with my clothes and shoes still on, and fell fast asleep. I stayed asleep until later that evening.

The Car Controversy

The next morning, my mom walked into my bedroom and tapped me on the head. For a minute I thought it was my brother playing with me like he always does, so I slapped her hand saying, "Stop Quincy." That's when my mom yells.

"Hey, get up! This isn't Quincy, this is your mother and whose car is that out there in my drive-way?"

I kept my eyes closed pretending to be asleep.

"Josie, I asked you whose car is that in my driveway?" she said for the second time, getting more upset.

I knew it was time to sit up and talk to her before she got upset and popped me upside the head for being disobedient.

"Floyd's," I answered her lazily.

"A man gives you his car to use…this must be getting serious."

"I think so." I answered shyly, not knowing what her reaction would be.

"Do you like him. I mean really like him?" she asked with such a serious look in her eyes that I knew I couldn't lie.

"I do mama. He's nice to me. Not once have we had a single argument.

He has never mistreated me and he promised he would never cheat or put his hands on me." I replied with such sincerity in my eyes and confidence in my tone.

"As long as he likes you and respects you the same way you like and respect him. It's all-good, but remember the one thing, you don't want to love a man more than he loves you, because the one who loves the most, is the one who usually gets hurt. Never give a man all of you; save a piece for yourself and never lose sight of reality. On that note, be careful, especially while driving around town in that man's car," she said just before she walked out of the door on her way to work.

"Have a good day mama," I replied with relief.

"Thank you pumpkin," My mom responded, with doubt in her voice, not knowing I was even listening at all. Only the future would tell.

I wasn't sure what she meant when she made the statement about loving someone more than they love you. I suppose it's a mama, thing or something she experienced when she was growing up; I would find out soon enough.

Cruising With My Girls

After mom left, I couldn't go back to sleep, so I paged my girlfriends and told them that I would be by to pick them up for lunch. I figured we could drive around town like some happy teenage girls having fun until Floyd paged me for his jeep . At this time I didn't even have a driver's license, so I was praying that the cops didn't pull me over and take me to jail, but that didn't stop us from enjoying ourselves.

I knew everybody went to "Mickey D's" for lunch, which was right the corner from our high school. I pulled into the Mickey D's and parked while acting silly and listening to music. We got out of the jeep and danced to certain songs with some of our other friends from school. Of course everyone thought Floyd's jeep was mine. Our next stop on our list was Arby's. We hung out for a few minutes before I dropped my girls back off to school. I decided to hang out alone, I wanted to gather my thoughts about my future with Floyd. All I could think about was how glad I was to just spend time with the girls. Not one person asked about Floyd; for that moment I felt like an innocent, sweet, mischievous teenage girl.

Floyd's Very First Fight

The Texas Station Casino parking lot was packed. This was a smaller casino in Vegas, not on the strip, but a popular casino for neighborhood gamblers. It was packed day and night, and on Fridays they had featured boxing matches that were aired on ESPN. It took my breath away when I saw the marquee, which was the last fight to be mentioned: "Floyd Mayweather vs. Roberto Apodaca." Underneath it said, "Mayweather Pro Debut," with a small picture of Floyd in a boxing pose. The other fights listed before his name looped again and ran across the screen, then above it his picture would appear. My 16-year-old heart started pounding. My mom and her best friend Monica attended the fight with me. Part of me felt as though my mom came simply to be nosey about the guy I was in love with, but I was happy she came nevertheless.

My man was a star! Millions would see his talent tonight! It was the first time I could picture him becoming a world champion one day. Seeing his name in lights made it all appear so real; his dream was about to come true for him. He was already well known for his Olympic medal and Golden Glove wins at that time. Leading up to this fight, Floyd said over and over that this was the one he needed to win to make it to the top. And he did. An announcer walked to Floyd with a microphone for an interview after his win. I sat very still in my seat with so many emotions running through my body—I even felt tears in my eyes. This was his moment. Mom, Monica and I went around to the side of the room and his uncle Roger brought us into Floyd's dressing room. There were a few reporters there.

"Hey, baby. Did you see me take care of that pussy?" he said as I approached him.

I ran over to him and hugged and kissed him.

"Now this is the kind of woman every man needs. She wants to hold me even when I'm sweaty and dirty," he said.

His smile lit up the room. I drifted off into a daydream at that moment, mind racing, thinking about how would this change our relationship. I couldn't let my thoughts get the best of me, so I tucked them away. I wanted this night to be about him.

The Thrill Is Over

Becoming Responsible

Floyd and I continued to spend lots of time together. I ended up renting a small apartment for myself, and Floyd lived in his two-bedroom house. I graduated from high school early and I knew it was time for me to become a woman and take-on adult responsibilities. My man came to my graduation and cheered for me as I walked across the stage with my diploma. I was happy when I looked up and Floyd was sitting in the audience with a bouquet of red roses. I chose to graduate early so I could dedicate more time to work.

I worked two jobs to pay for my apartment and to help my mom. Also, I took online college courses. When I ran short of money, I danced at a topless bar a couple nights a month to make ends meet. Floyd hated my dancing gig, but I had no choice at the time. He wasn't making enough money to support the both of us. Not to mention, I earned between five hundred and one thousand dollars each night. Right or wrong, I refused to give up my third job because it paid the most, and it was the extra money I needed to pay for my education. I think my work ethic and sacrifice inspired Floyd to continue his dream. He wanted me to be strong, and he was always supportive of my actions, helping me in any way he could. I would later find out that I was not the only person he was supporting at that time.

The one thing I did inherit from mom was her work ethic. I never doubted myself when it was time to grow up and become a responsible woman. I was never afraid of hard work and working long hours. Even though I didn't care for dancing at the topless club, I knew it would be temporary and it would help me accomplish my goals. Other women made themselves available for 'happy endings' for some of the customers. That was the one thing I promised myself I would never do. I would never offer myself up for a monetary exchange. How could I be in a committed relationship while giving my body to strangers, simply because they had more money than my man did. No way in hell would I stoop that low.

During this time of learning how to be responsible, I was striving to be a woman of her word. I wanted to exhibit kindness to everyone I met. Kindness went a long way in the dancing business. I was also teaching myself to be what I believed a good, wholesome wife would be, in preparation for when Floyd proposed to me.

I needed to demonstrate to him that I was the one. The one who would have his back regardless of the situation. The one who would lie to the police or district attorney for him if needed. The one who would kick her shoes off and the fight if he was being jumped. The one who would stand by him if things became tough. The one who would take care of him if he became injured or disabled. That was my mission.

Sometimes I wish took a shortcut, but I had no one there to help guide me on my path. I took matters into my own hands and made lots of mistakes along the way. But I learned that mistakes were a part of real life in the real world. We must all go through ups and downs to appreciate the good. While I was becoming an adult, it seemed Floyd was becoming a man-child.

Ex-Boyfriend Drama

"What the fuck are you telling your new boyfriend?" Tony's voice screamed through my phone.

"Tony?" I asked, "what are you talking about?"

"Floyd ran up on me last night, forced me off the road, pulled me out of the car, and punched me. The nigga threatened me and told me to stay away from you. What the hell are you telling this motha fucka? I haven't seen you in over a year!"

"I have no idea what you're talking about Tony!" I answered.

"Did you say something to him?"

"I didn't say anything about you to him," I answered.

"I don't even know how he found me. How does he know what type of car I drive? I'm not his sparring partner. You better tell that nigga to stop fuckin with me Josie."

"Are you seeing his old girlfriend Melissa again?" I asked.

I thought this might surprise him. Floyd and I figured out a few weeks ago that our exes had dated each other at one point in time.

"Who are you talking about?" Tony said, playing dumb.

"One of those girls you were seeing when I thought you were being loyal to me was one of Floyd's exes," I answered.

"Like I said, tell that nigga to leave me the fuck alone!" he said angrily and hung up.

 I immediately cleared my line and dialed Floyd's cell phone. His voice mail answered so I left him a message.

"Floyd, I just got a call from my ex Tony and he said that you tried to run him off the road and jumped him, what's up with that? I've got nothing to do with him and you know that. Call me later."

Shortly after, Floyd called back.

"I got your message. I wanted to send that punk-ass ex-boyfriend of yours a message to stay away from you. You're mine; I'm the only one for you. Remember that!"

After that situation, my relationship with Floyd was good, his career was moving up, I was still working hard and figuring out what I wanted out in life. I knew one thing for sure: I loved Floyd with all my heart and I couldn't wait till we could start a family. Time went by and we found out we were pregnant. I thought he might freak out or get upset, but he was happy too. A new chapter was about to begin.

Giving Birth: Welcome to Motherhood

On November 17, 1999, I gave birth to my first child, a beautiful son. We named him Koraun Mayweather. We were afraid and filled with joy at the same time. What a joy it was to hold my son in my arms; my heart had never felt this much emotion. There are no words to explain the feelings I experienced when I became a mother.

Both Floyd and I were proud parents. Believe it or not, that was the first day I truly felt like someone special; to bring a life into the world is a feeling you cannot know unless you've experienced it. I vowed to myself to treasure my son and do everything I could to give him the best life possible. I continued to work my jobs, and take my online classes. Being a young mother it had its challenges, but I made it work; I had a new motivation to keep me from giving up.

Floyd would sometimes watch the baby when I went to work, and he did what he could when it came to buying things for our son. Now that we were parents, we had to grow up and leave our childlike ways in the past. Running the street, hanging out with the boys, and staying out late had to slow down. I had this conversation with him a few times but he wasn't listening.

Sometimes I wondered if Floyd only wanted to get me pregnant so he could claim me as his own, making sure I would never leave him. The two of us were irresponsible having sex with no protection, but is it really Floyd's fault? I was prescribed birth control pills but I found myself forgetting to take them and not suggesting we use a condom. That was part of me was being irresponsible; I knew better, but sometimes I got caught up in the moment.

I think in back of my mind I was ready to be a mother, but I did not want to be a statistic. Having a child out of wedlock, waiting on a welfare check, and food stamps each month were in not my plans. Of course, it's too late now, my son is here and I'm a proud mother. My job now is to be the best mom I can possibly be. Even if I have to work five jobs, my son will never go without food, clean clothes, or a roof over his head.

As time went on I realized how hard it was to be a single parent. Even though Floyd would come by to hang out and spend time, he still had his own place. It wasn't like we were living under the same roof and splitting the bills; it felt different knowing we were not truly a family. It had only been a few days since I was released from the hospital when I received a call from one of my girlfriends.

The Other Woman

It was a Thursday afternoon when the phone rang.

"Hey girl. What's up and how is the baby?"

"Me and the baby are great. How are you?" I asked.

"I'm good. No complaints."

"Good for you. So, when are you joining the baby club?" I asked jokingly.

"Me? Having a baby? That's not in my plans girl. I'm too young for a baby. Besides, what would I do with a baby when I'm a baby myself? Speaking of babies, I got a call from a reliable source who told me that your man, Floyd, got some other woman pregnant."

"That's bull-shit! I don't believe it; we just had a baby," I responded.

"That's the word on the street. I heard she's around three months pregnant."

"If this is all true, do you have a name?" I asked.

"Her name I believe is Melissa."

"M-e-l-i-s-s-a? That's Floyd ex. This can't be true. I can't believe it. Let me get off the phone before I lose it. I'll call you later. I need to get in touch with Floyd right fuckin' now."

I quickly dialed Floyd's number. No answer. I paged him at least fifty times and still no answer. My son started crying because he was hungry and needed to be changed. Meanwhile, I cried like a newborn baby, devastated and confused by the information I had just received. The mere the thought of him getting his ex pregnant was mind blowing. I would never do that to the one I love. This was the ultimate betrayal.

Our son was only a few days old. What the hell was he thinking? Or was he? I used to hear stories of men who would go off and fuck another woman after his wife gave birth. A woman usually has to wait for the six-week check-up (sometimes longer) and the man acts like he can't wait. But if she was already three months pregnant, I was still pregnant too. Even though it was only a rumor at this point, I was still so embarrassed.

Floyd finally called me back.

"What's up Josie?" Floyd asked when I picked up.

"I heard some bull shit from my girl."

"What is it this time I had some bitch in my car or someone saw me out eating at a restaurant with some chick?"

"No, I wish it was one of those things. The rumor around town is that you got your friend Melissa pregnant; the same bitch I asked if you were fuckin back when we first met at the bowling alley. I hope it isn't true Floyd. I'm due with our son in three months. That would be fucked-up. How could you?" I almost couldn't get all my words out without the tears falling.

Floyd denied having seen or spoken with Melissa since we got together. Should I believe him or should I believe the rumor on the street? Ninety-nine percent of the time the streets don't lie, but my heart wanted to believe him, to believe I was his only girl and the only one with his child. I chose to be a responsible adult in the situation: I decided to wait for another six months to see if the truth would come to light. In the meantime, I gave Floyd the benefit of the doubt, knowing how people could lie and spread false rumors.

I hung the phone up, changed our son, prepared his food, and started to prepare dinner for Floyd and myself, since he mentioned he was coming over to spend a few nights at my place. I suppose I took it like a woman and tried to not let it bother me. I didn't want to give up my trust for him without the facts, because that would be hard to get over. I decided to…

It's Challenging Being An Adult

Fame and Infidelity

The first few years it was just Floyd and me. But when he got a contract to fight in the big league, he started changing. He became a man I have never seen before. He began to cheat on me—or at least this was when he was officially caught. The disrespect toward me began in a way I would never have imagined. The arguments were excruciating and made me so confused and upset. I remember checking him for talking to another woman and he slapped the hell out of me.

In that moment I froze. So many thoughts were rumbling through my head. Do I hit him back? Do I run away? Do I scream and show my pain? Do I hide and show nothing? Do I leave? Do I stay? Why was this decision so hard? Shouldn't I just know what to do? I missed my mom in that moment and wish I had my dad to comfort me too. I was too embarrassed to call my mom, too afraid to mention it to my brother, and too ashamed to tell my best friend. This was the first time he had ever hit me, and it should have been the last, but I had already fallen in love with the devil.

They say love is blind and they're right. I kept a blindfold over my eyes for years, allowing Floyd to be the player he wanted to be. Of course it wasn't until he had become a millionaire that he really changed. He was just a regular street dude who had a dream of becoming a professional boxer and his dream came true. No matter how much money he made, he didn't gain class or integrity. You can take a man out of the hood but you can't take the hood out of the man. Floyd will never change his ways. He's a fool with money.

Fame

Life got c-r-a-z-y and changed drastically, both for the better and worse. When Floyd and I first met we were both broke teenagers in love—full of dreams like fairytales. The minute he became famous, things went from good, to bad, to ugly. A new attitude developed; we spent less and less time together and he became too busy to answer the phone.

They say a fool and his money will depart. I believe that, but I also believe that it's okay for people to have money and lots of it. However fools and money don't go well together. Take a wild animal out of the jungle and it will run wild in confusion. The same occurs when a fool obtains lots of money: he doesn't know how to act. I wish we could start all over again. I wish I could take away his fame. When you allow money to cause you to look down on people, and you want everyone to look up at you, that's a problem. How easy it is for people to forget where they came from, to forget the days of trying to scrounge some coins together to get something to eat? If asked what I really think about fools and money my answer would be: self-destruction. It's only a matter of time until stupidity takes over for the win.

Cheaters

All I ever wanted was a man who wanted me for me; to love me, honor me, and to only be with me. My first boyfriend cheated, my second boyfriend cheated, and my Floyd cheated. Was I a cheater magnet? What did I do wrong? What makes a man cheat? Well, I now know it wasn't my fault, but most women we tend to blame themselves.

In my own opinion and experience, men cheat for multiple reasons. Some men do what they saw their father doing: juggling women acting like it's acceptable. It's like a game to them—chase the cat until you catch her; but in the end, he only wants one thing. The harder the chase, the more exciting it is. He'll wine and dine until she gives in, then take what he wants. He'll be kind and respectful until she gives him what he desires, then it's on to the next.

Some cheaters aren't looking for an easy one-night-stand; this type of cheater wants to master his game by believing he could have any woman he wants. Some cheaters simply want to have as many sexual encounters with as many different women as possible. A cheater comes in all types of disguises and can be very elusive. Some are poor and some are rich. Some are attractive some are not. But they're all good manipulators. Sadly, you just don't know until you're in a relationship with a cheater.

Bottom line, take your time and don't rush into a relationship. Your partner should be your best friend and wants what you want in a relationship and in life. A few signs to look for when trying to spot a cheater (keeping in mind that some are better than others): A cheater will never tell you all the information about a situation; a cheater will never volunteer information and when they give you information, it will usually be short and simple. A cheater will hide their phone or keep it with them at all times; a cheater will have a password on their device, always placing the device upside down so you cannot see the screen, keeping notifications private; and will hesitate to use it in your presence. A cheater will not offer you to come along to family gathering, hanging out with friends, or business trips; most cheaters choose to have a different place to stay, even when the relationship is serious, because they need that freedom to do as they please and not get caught. They can become less affectionate towards you and their sexual behavior might change; they care more about how they look when they are leaving the house without you than when going somewhere with you; they try to buy you gifts and do little sweet things to make you think you are still special; they may come around less, call less, be less kind, lie more, and change plans without warning.

Some women may not care that their man cheats and that is okay, as long as they're happy. Not all women want the same things, but if you know you don't want a cheater, keep your eyes open and your heart in check.

Wanna Be a Trophy Wife?

This life isn't for everyone and for those young girls and women who are chasing the dream of becoming a "trophy wife," they should really think twice. In many cases, the price of this position will cost you your self-respect, self-worth, or even your life. Trying to become famous by being with some guy is for the birds. Most men only want one thing, like the lyrics to Lauryn Hills hit single, "That Thing. Trophy wives or girlfriends are often cheated on, disrespected, mentally and physically abused, and end up suffering fro a broken heart.

A beating for a designer handbag or a fancy car for being choked to near death is not a fair trade in my opinion. You're worth cannot be measured by a handbag, a car, or any material item. My mistake was that I became too dependent on Floyd to provide for me when in hindsight, I should've stayed in school, got a career, and made my own damn money. Most men with lots of money will buy you material things to get you to like them, and once you buy into it and get you hooked they'll treat you like shit. If you are unwilling to perform all of their sexual desires in bed, it's a strike against you. At that point you're just a pretty face with a sexy body, which means nothing when all is said and done. Believe me. Take it from a woman that took enough blows mentally and physically for a lifetime.

Be stronger than me. Don't be afraid to walk away and to tell someone that you're being abused. Someone will hear you and hopefully your truth can save someone else from a similar story. I hope every young girl and woman's spirit hears my voice. Your story does not have to end up like mine.

Cheating Impacts The Famous And Infamous

STD

Being a player sometimes comes with a price; and that price can cost you your life. Floyd's playing has cost him many times over. On several occasions, we found ourselves sitting in the clinic, waiting to see a doctor, to get another shot or a 14-day prescription to clear up another sexually transmitted disease. Whenever I addressed these dirty and embarrassing cycles, he became violent towards me, and at times even accused me of being the one at fault, knowing he was the who contracted first.

"If you're going to fuck those street bitches then at least protect yourself and me!" I shouted out to him as I ran out the door; "One day you're going to catch something that you can't get rid of. You may not mind dying, just don't take me with you!"

When I contracted an STD, I was so ashamed I couldn't even tell my best friend. It left me feeling dirty, tainted, and unattractive. I didn't speak to Floyd for a week and it was hard for me to forgive him, especially when it was a recurring thing. After going through all the bullshit and the lies, I found out I was pregnant for the second time. I believed maybe this baby would bring us closer together.

March 28, 2001 I gave birth to my second son, Zion Shamaree Mayweather. Another happy moment in my life. I was a mother for the second time and so grateful that I had a healthy and happy baby. Maybe I had another child to remind me of the true love I was lacking from Floyd. I had two beautiful sons now who needed me, so I needed to do my best to take care of them the best way I knew how. I promised to give them all the love they needed and more, and to make sure they never wanted for anything in the world. I devoted the majority of my time to being a damn good mother, if nothing else.

Consent Rape

Ninety percent of the time when he wanted sex, I gave it to him, and I did so without complaint. One night, Floyd was out all night long, and when he came home to me sleeping in my bed, minding my own business, he decided that he wanted some. He didn't even wake me up for consent. When you take something from someone, it's called stealing and invading privacy. On this particular night, he took what he wanted from me without asking. I felt like he enjoyed it because it became a common occurrence. In fact, I believe he felt gratification from taking what he wanted, how and where he wanted, despite my lack of consent. He was a bully who enjoyed beating down the weak for his own personal enjoyment.

I had only been asleep for a few hours before he came into the bedroom and ripped my t-shirt and panties off and started to put his penis inside of me. It was terrible and unbearable because I was dry and wasn't in the mood, but that did not matter to him.

"What are you doing Floyd?" I asked.

"You know what I'm doing."

"Stop, I'm not in the mood and I'm not feeling well. Stop, I'm serious, get off me" I begged him.

It was like talking to the wall. He took my body like it was his property. There was no warning of his intentions. That night I felt for all the women who had been victimized and raped in their life. Society can make you feel that you can't be made a rape victim by someone you're in a relationship with. As I got older, I noticed that Floyd got a kick out taking things and taking advantage of people who loved him. He'd disrespect people and often used his money to control, manipulate, and demean others. Any time a man has sex with his wife, girlfriend, his side chick, or anyone who expressed the word "no," his act is automatically known as rape. Having sex must to be consensual for all parties, no matter who you are.

Am I Losing My Mind?

Floyd has had several physical assaults on four women besides me, for which he was arrested and received a citation. I still can't believe he had the nerve to enter the ring before each fight to music bashing women. Thirty days after the Corrales fight, he got into a huge argument (one of many) with his ex, Melissa Brim, the mother of Floyd's daughter, Ayanna, over child support. I heard that Floyd beat the shit out of her. I came to realize that it wasn't just me he abused, and that it might never end. Several months later in March 2002, Floyd pleaded guilty and received a suspended sentence with no jail time. While I sit here thinking about the past and everything that went wrong, there was one good thing that came from all this. On June 25, 2003 I gave birth to my third and last child, Jirah Mayweather. Let me take you back.

At this point, I'm sure Floyd thought he was Mr. Untouchable. August 2003, Floyd and a few of his boys were at the Ra nightclub at the Luxor in

Las Vegas when he ran into two of my girlfriends, Herneatha and Karra. Floyd never liked Herneatha. They noticed him coming their way so they decided to leave the club to avoid him. Floyd got closer to them and before they knew what was happening, Floyd punched her in the left side of her jaw and punched Karra in the back of her head. Herneatha tried to run but she was punched again, causing her to fall to the ground. My girl Karra tried to help, but Floyd hit her again. After that he ran out of the club like a coward.

Later, when I called Floyd to find out why he did what he did, he said, "I never approved of you having friends like them." When did I ever need his approval to have friends? I knew then he was a little 51/50. My girlfriends filed charges against Floyd. June 2003, Floyd was found guilty on two accounts of battery and (again) received a suspended sentence with no jail time. Early 2005 his guilty verdict was vacated.

Later in 2005, Floyd and I got into it in front of the parking lot of SRO. He and I were sitting in his Bentley talking. I confronted him for the way he was acting towards another woman. Same ole thing over and over again, but it still pissed me off because of how much love I had for him. This time he got so damn mad, he punched me, kicked me, then jumped out of the car, ran around to open the passenger door, grabbed me by my hair and dragged me to the ground causing a facial laceration. When I filed the police report the officer asked me if Floyd had beat me before and of course I told him yes, too many times to count.

By the time the trial started July 2005, I changed my story to protect him and his career, pushing my feelings to the side. I told the prosecutor that it was me who started the fight and I was totally out of control, so he grabbed me by my arms to get me out of his car. I even told the prosecutor that Floyd would never hit or kick me. "He's like a teddy bear inside." Why didn't I have the courage then to do what was right and put a stop to this once and for all? What a fool I was back then. Of course he was acquitted and all charges dropped against him. He had a way of making up for my good deed. He purchased a $500,000 25-carat diamond ring, took me out to dinner, and apologized. I forgave him, but it didn't last long.

Broken Promises

It was the summer of 2006; Floyd and I were at home watching television when my cell phone rang. I looked over at the phone and recognized the number. It was my girlfriend. I answered.

"Hello?"

"Hey girl what are you doing?"

"Sitting here watching a movie with my boo. What's up?"

"G-i-r-l! I am sorry to have to tell you this but your Boo is messin' around on you!"

"How do you know?" I asked, I got up and walked into the other room.

"The girl he's messin with is a good friend of my best friend's sister who lives around the corner from my mama's house. Besides, I saw him with her last night at the casino with my own eyes and my eyes don't lie."

"What's her name?" I asked, though a part of me didn't really want to know.

"Her name is… don't tell him I told you. You know he don't like me."

"Thanks girl. I'll call you back later. I need to confront this motha fucka!"

I hung up the phone and walked back into the living room where Floyd was watching TV. I grabbed the remote and turned the television off. I stood in front of him with my hands on my hips. He looked up at me,

"What's up?" he said.

At that time all I could do was cry. I guess the combination of anger and hurt got the best of me. I reached over and picked up a glass of water I had been drinking and threw it across the room; it hit the wall, broke, and then I screamed out…

"Why Floyd why!! What did I ever do to you!?"

"Why what?" he said, sitting there with that funny look on his face— the same look he had when he lied about other bitches.

"I suspected you were cheating on me again! I just could never put my finger on it. You ain't shit! You're nothing but a lying ass-hole! You're just like all the other men that cheat! I saw it coming. The more fame you got, the more money you made, the more you changed! A man with new money and fame cannot be trusted. I suppose everything I heard growing up is true. The kids and I are moving out! You can have this house and those tramps!" I said as I ran upstairs to the bedroom to pack.

Floyd jumped up and followed me to the bedroom. He was talking to me at the same time.

"Come on baby don't do this. You know I love you and I'm not going to let you take my kids. Hell nah! That shit you heard about me is bull-shit baby. I haven't cheated on you since Melissa. You gotta believe me."

I stopped, and turned around.

"So you did cheat on me with that tramp? But I already knew that, in case you forgot, you guys have a child together! You're nothing but a dog Floyd!"

"Okay I fucked Melissa, but she never meant nothin' to me."

"And neither did I! Why do you think you can go around fuckin every woman you see when you have a woman at home? Then you expect me to believe that it doesn't matter because 'she don't mean anything to me'? Give me a fuckin break Floyd!"

"Where are you and the kids going?" he questioned in a demanding tone.

"I'm getting far away from your ass!" I screamed as tears still ran down my face.

"I wanna know where you are taking my kids!"

"I'm moving to California. I'm not going to stay here in Vegas where you got another woman pregnant!"

"You don't know if she's pregnant and if she is you don't know if it's mine." Floyd said.

I stopped and turned around and looked at him for a moment in silence.

"You just can't help yourself. At least I can thank you for the truth, or at least half of the truth, Floyd."

I started packing my things while he stood there trying to figure out how to get out of the shit he stepped in.

"This is no longer working for me. That was the last straw Floyd. I can't do this anymore. I'm done! You hurt me over and over and my heart can no longer take it. I'm going to mess around and have a damn heart attack at the age of twenty-five. The sad part is I heard you have been messing with this one for three years. Is she pregnant too?" I asked him

"No, ain't nobody pregnant."

"Now I know why you kept running your ass back and forth to Florida.

'I had business to take care of is what you kept telling me when all along the business was another woman you were seeing. You weren't man enough to tell me the truth?" I asked.

"It's not true baby. You gotta believe me."

All Floyd did was lie and I knew he was lying this time. Just as I suspected years ago when he lied about Melissa being pregnant six months after I gave birth to our first son, Melissa gave birth to a baby girl; which we later found out through DNA testing was Floyd's. I still can't believe I forgave him and gave him chance after chance.

On June 23, 2006, I rented a truck and hired movers to pack up me and my kids and our things, and we got the hell out of Vegas. The next morning we were in the city of Valencia, where I rented a house. We lived there for two years before the owner of the house decided to move back in, giving us a 30-day notice to move out. Floyd heard about that happening and offered for us to stay with him instead of trying to find somewhere else to live. When the kids and I moved back to Vegas, we moved in with him until I could find a home. I didn't want to, but I didn't know what other choice I had. The kids missed him and I can't lie, part of me missed him too. Maybe the fantasy of us living as a family living under one roof gave me some hope. But Floyd would always say one thing and do another, so I had to stay on my toes.

Sucker For Love

Tina Marie had a hit song called "I'm Just a Sucker for Your Love," and that was definitely me. Whatever Floyd asked I did, whatever he told me to do, I went along with it. I didn't know how to say no to him and the love was so strong, I didn't want to say no. I breathed for him at night and I lived for him in the day. There was nothing that could come between us. We were like white on rice, peanut butter and jelly, and milk and cookies. I used to ask myself how I got to that point? How did I fall in love and when did I fall so deep? Finding my way out seemed impossible to me. It's like drowning in quicksand: No one can save you and you can't save yourself. Was this how I was going to feel until the end of my life? Even when I found the strength to pull myself up, he always found a way to push me back into that quicksand. All I wanted was to be loved and happy until the day I die. But sadly, I never received the love from the man I fell for at 16 years old, and happiness was not part of my story with Floyd.

Protecting Yourself Is Your Responsibility

Things Are Falling Apart

Its 7:40 in the morning and my cell phone rings. It's one of my girlfriends telling me about some Instagram photos of Floyd and another woman. It was that very moment when I hung up the phone that I had had enough. I'm decided to pack my things and the kids to move to Los Angeles. At this time I had no idea what part of LA I would go to, but anywhere would do at that point. I just couldn't do Vegas any more.

I started making plans for my move with the kids, but I knew I had to tell him that I was taking the kids with me. I was willing to bet all I had that this conversation wasn't going to go well. I knew how he felt about our children and I couldn't just take them away without some type of child custody battle because he was a good dad. I prepared myself for what was coming when I had to call him. I got dressed and headed to a nearby restaurant to get something to eat before picking up the kids. As I sat there alone gathering my intimate thoughts, three young women walked into the restaurant and took a seat; I couldn't help overhearing their conversation. They were loud.

One of these women I knew. I had had a previous encounter with her regarding messing around with Floyd, and here she was talking about how she had hung out with him the night before. They all giggled and high-fived. I tried to relax and enjoy my meal, but their continuous loud talk made it hard for me and I just couldn't take it anymore. In a previous conversation with this woman, I told her to leave my man alone, but it didn't seem like she got the memo.

Even though I was planning to move, and I told myself I shouldn't care about this other woman, it was hard to control myself. I didn't want to see him with anyone else. So without thinking, I got up, walked over to the woman who was doing all of the talking and hit her on the back of her head with my fist. Her face fell straight into her grits and eggs. One of the other two looked up at me and shouted out.

"What's wrong with you bitch?

"Your girl got a big mouth and she talks too much" I said.

"Why did you hit her?" said the other woman.

"I told this bitch a few weeks ago to leave my man alone, that's why" I responded.

The woman I punched raised up to wipe the food from her face. She jumped up as if she was going to hit me, so I punched her again in the nose, but before I could get in my fighting position, I could see blood running down her face. She stood there holding her nose while her girlfriends tried to stop the bleeding with napkins. The owner of the restaurant ran over to stop the fight, or should I say to stop me from giving her a natural beat down.

"Hey what in the hell are you doing? You need to take that ratchet behavior somewhere else before I call the police and have you all sent to jail" the owner said.

The three women picked up their purses and headed out the front door. I too got my handbag and left. Due to the commotion, the owner forgot to ask any of us to pay our tab. This is how my day began, and it was just getting started.

That shit was making me crazy by the minute. Here I was, fighting over a man that clearly didn't want anything to do with me, at least not in a committed relationship. I really needed to ask myself: Why allow him to take me to this level? I looked like a crazy, no class ghetto woman that needed some home training, when I was truly just a woman confused, in love, and trying to escape.

After leaving the restaurant, I decided to go to the mall and buy myself something. I needed to clear my mind. I shopped for half of the day and then made my way to pick up my kids. As we walked through the door my son yelled,

"Hey mom, what's for dinner?"

The phone rings, its Floyd.

"Let me speak with your dad for a moment, go have a snack and I will make you guys something when I get off the phone, or we can go out to eat."

"Okay mom."

I made my way to my bedroom because I did not want the kids to hear me arguing with their father. Even though they'd heard us argue before, I didn't want them to see it coming from me when I had a chance to do the right thing. I shut the bedroom door behind and sat on the edge of the bed.

"I got your message about moving to L.A. What's up with that?

"I cannot do this anymore Floyd. I'm waking up to phone calls about you and some other bitch; I'm in the streets jumping on bitches because my man is cheating on me. Enough is enough and the kids are moving to

Los Angeles."

"Baby, come on."

"Baby my ass, I'm tired of being your fool. You treat the whores like they're your main women and I'm the side chick. How much more do you want me to take? I asked him.

"You know I love you and only you."

"You have a weird way of showing it. The things you have done to me, I wouldn't do to my worst enemy. Let me remind you in case your memory has failed you. You had another child with your ex, while dating me. You've cheated on me with other tramps and whores. You gave me STDs, not once, but several times. You beat the shit out of me so many times I lost count. You have embarrassed me in front of my friends, family, and our children. You bought me gifts and took them back when you got mad at me. You threatened to kill the kids and me that night you beat me half to death. Should I go on?" I asked him.

For the next 30-seconds it was dead silence. I'm sure he had to gather his thoughts and figure out what bullshit line he would feed me this time.

"You know I love you Josie," he said for the hundredth time.

"Bye, Floyd.

"You're not taking my kids."

"Watch me." I responded as I hung up the phone.

Two Weeks Later

The kids and I moved from Vegas to Los Angeles. We settled into our new place, a place I hoped I would find happiness and peace of mind.

One Year Later

The kids and I started to miss Floyd. I understood why the kids missed him, he's their father, but why couldn't I get him out of my head? He and I started having long conversations a few times a day. It started to feel like the good ole' days. My heart would skip beats when he would say how much he loved and missed me. He'd remind me of the good times we had as a couple and as a family. I started to feel like the break was good for us, and that he really did miss us and want to be a family. After a few months of sweet-talking he convinced me to gather my things and move back to Vegas with the kids. I must admit that was one of the happiest days of my life I finally had hope that my dreams were going to come true.

Floyd had purchased a home for our family; and told me he put the house in a trust fund for the kids. Finally it looked like God had answered my prayers. But it wasn't long before Floyd was back to his old games, or maybe I just opened my eyes back up to the bullshit. As much as I wanted to believe he had changed, there was still a little doubt in my mind. Over and over again he lied to me during our years together, but the last thing I ever thought he would do was lie to our children. Later I found out that the house he purchased was never put into a trust. Instead, the house was placed in one of his corporations. I asked myself: Why would a man who has so much not want to leave something to his children?

My House Is Not A Home

I remember nights just sitting around watching movies on Netflix and talking to my girlfriends on the phone, wishing Floyd was with me. He was traveling and training, sometimes 18-hours a day, so he spent very

86

little time with the kids and me. Even though we lived in a big beautiful house, it never felt like a home. Love and partnership is what makes a house feel like a home. It's funny, every time I hear that Luther Vandross song "A house is Not a Home," I tear up because it reminds me of this time in my life. I felt so alone. Of course I had the kids to play with, but it's not the same as having a partner to spend time with. I missed cuddling, watching movies, playing cards, watching the stars, etc. What kept me from going insane were my children, family, and friends. I understand now how some of these rich women feel. They live in $20-million mansions with a maid, housekeeper, butler, private chef, and all the money in the world, but they still feel lonely as hell. This is not what I signed up for. I wanted a family and home, not just a house for my family to live in.

Gossip, Gossip, Gossip

One afternoon Floyd and I were hanging out at the park. I brought up a topic most men hate discussing: The other woman. It's hard to overlook or refrain from listening when you hear gossip about the one you love being involved with someone else. I asked Floyd about a girl that my best friend Bernice told me about. This girl supposedly followed him from Grand Rapids.

"I have a question?" I asked Floyd.

"What's your question?"

"My girlfriend told me about this girl that followed you here from Grand Rapids. What's up with that?"

"I see, so this girlfriend of yours loves to gossip. What's her name again, Bernice?"

"Yeah that's her name." I replied.

"Well, Bernice needs to get some business of her own and stay the fuck out of mine. She is my friend from high school and she came to Las Vegas to visit like everybody else does. She stayed a few days and went back to Grand Rapids."

"That doesn't mean you didn't have sex with her!" I snarled back.

"Sex! Is that why you are asking me these questions? Can't a man be a friend with a female without having sex with them? Damn!"

"Did you or didn't you have sex with her?"

"No, I didn't have sex with her, she is just my home-girl. Don't get caught up with gossip Josie," Floyd said, starting to get irritated.

"What do you mean by don't get caught up?" I replied while giving him the side eye.

"Like I said, don't get caught up with the 'he said, she said' bullshit. Anyway Josie, as far as I'm concerned, you're the finest woman in Las Vegas. I can't get caught up just because some other dude holla at you. You have to realize that when a man or woman are attractive, people are going to look, check them out, and maybe even flirt. That comes with the territory."

"Alright but what about your other baby mama, Melissa, how do I know she is still not trying to get back with you. Maybe you gave in and gave her some action too!"

"Did your girlfriend talk about her too? Anyway, that's old news, we're together tonight and that's what counts, Josie."

Floyd looked at me with his soft brown eyes. Man, he is so irresistible I thought. He did something I had seen before: He changed the subject and started talking about his boxing career.

"When I was in the Olympics in Atlanta last year I got screwed out of the Gold Medal. The US tried to get the gold for me, the decision was disrupted, they disputed, and the referee was shocked when the winner was announced. Them motha fuckas! I still can't even believe it. Even the Olympics are fixed! It's all-political. But we brought home the Bronze, and this situation taught me a big lesson. In order to guarantee a win you gotta knock that sucka out!" He laughed out loud. You know that I just signed with Top Rank and Bob Arum? They said I'd never have to worry about anything again. They are going to take me straight to the top!"

I smiled before I asked him the next silly question, "What's Top Rank?"

"They manage boxers who are going pro."

"That sounds great, but do you feel like you will be able to trust them? I only ask because I've always heard that boxing is corrupt."

"I heard the same thing but what can I do about it," he replied, shrugging his shoulders.

"Just be careful and make sure that you have a damn good attorney and an accountant on your side. I'd hate to see you end up broke like a lot of other boxers," I told him.

"How do you know who to trust?" Floyd asked, throwing his arms up in the air.

"How do you ever know?"

I thought about how many times I had trusted people only to learn they weren't honest or trustworthy at all.

Floyd reached over and raised my head up and said, "You can trust me. For one thing, I'm not Bernice. She's a messy whore and she doesn't mean you no good."

"Stop it!" We laughed together.

"I'm talking about that real trust. The kind-of-trust when you know that a person really' got your back."

"Do you trust your Uncle Roger over your father?"

"I trust Uncle Roger when it comes down to training me. My dad always wanted to control everyone and everything around him. If it didn't go his way, he wouldn't approve. My dad used to be both my manager and my trainer. He made all the decisions. My job was to go out and box. When it came to any of my ideas, they didn't mean shit to him. When I was younger, some of my ideas mattered a little to him, because he was trying to be a decent father, but now that I'm older and able to make my own decisions, he has a problem with it," Floyd said.

I nodded my head in agreement.

"Do you hate your father? Because you never say anything good about him," I asked, hoping to finally get some answers.

"Hell yeah!" Floyd shouted, as he jumped up in frustration. I suppose that was his way of dealing with the pain and the hurt he felt from dad. After seeing how angry he got, I kept my questions to myself when it came to his father. I knew that was a very touchy subject, one he didn't want to talk about because he never gave many details.

"Did you love your mom?" I asked, thinking about how he treated the women in his life, including me. I was curious.

"Of course I did, but sometimes I wonder if she loved us. It seemed as if the only thing that was important to her was dope. She put that shit before her own kids. Thank God I had sisters who cared about me. My older sister was the one that raised us when my mom was missing in action."

Floyd became emotional. I reached over and held him tightly. That was all I could do. I could feel the pain he was feeling.

"I'm sorry you had to go through all of that growing up. I went through the same thing with my parents. My life was no better than yours, believe me. I believe we have a lot in common. Maybe God brought us together to fill that void we have in our lives."

Those voids eventually became bonds between us. We both made a vow to never be like our parents. While holding Floyd, all I could think about was kissing him. His lips were like marshmallows, soft and spongy, and so irresistible. Before I knew it, I reached over and took his hand and wrapped it around my neck. I leaned over and kissed him. I looked at his pretty dark- brown eyes to see his reaction. He was shocked, and before I knew it, bam! Love is body language, not standing still. I knew that I should leave this man alone but he was so addictive; I was an addict for Floyd. I welcomed love every day of the week, and twice on Sundays. I loved him so much that somehow my brain could void out the bad and make me feel the same as I did in the very beginning. He started to squeeze my hand and his touch drew me closer to him. Then I had a quick reality check, and pulled away from him. I wiped my wet lips, looked at him and said,

"It's too much. We gotta stop playing ourselves. I know you will always hurt me, it always happens. It's not right. I can't."

"No, no, no! You know you're mine Josie," he said.

I noticed that the sun was just coming up—no wonder I was so tired.

I laid my head against his shoulder and he put his arms around me…I felt protected when we were together. I told a friend once if we were in a forest and a 500 lb. bear was coming toward me, Floyd would fight to the death to protect me. But that was in the beginning.

We kissed and held each other tightly. After a few minutes, Floyd drove me home. Another day, another night, and another kiss. I realized during our discussion about Bernice's gossip that I needed to keep my mouth shut when I heard things about him. Women are going to flirt with him just like men flirt with me. If I go around assuming that every time he's with a girl that they're having sex, I'll be crazy before I reach the age of 40. Of course, that's easier said than done when you're in love and he's done it before. Hell, it's been fifteen years and I still don't listen to everything I hear. I learned something at the park that afternoon, and that was to leave the gossip to Enquire and TMZ.

Broken Trust

As our lives became more complex I would often find myself thinking back on those carefree moments like the days in the park. I'd find myself wondering if there was something I could have done to prevent the lack of trust that developed in our relationship. How could two people be so in love, from the very first time they met, yet end up not trusting each other?

I remember when Floyd and I used to sit around and talk about unconditional love. We talked about the love neither one of us really had growing up. Deep inside, I always knew that unconditional love was what we both needed is kids. Unfortunately, life didn't come with instructions or a handbook to show us how to deal with our emotions in troubled times.

Neither of us knew how to deal with the jealousy, the fame, the money, and the greed. We were teenagers in love. We went with the flow and we were living in the moment. We thought we were invincible when we were together. Well at least that's the way I felt when I was in his arms or in his presence. I can still recall the Saturday afternoon when the trust we had built over the years began to fall apart. Floyd was in the living room watching one of his old fights when I walked over and sat down beside him.

"How are you feeling baby?" I asked as I reached out and held his hand.

"I'm cool. How are you feeling?"

"I'm okay."

"Good."

Then I stared at him for a few minutes before saying another word.

Then I said, "Baby, You know I trust you with all my heart don't you?"

"Yeah, I know that."

"And you know I love you even down to your dirty underwear's?"

"I know that too. What's up?"

"I have a question to ask you. I heard a rumor this afternoon about you."

"That's nothing new," he replied, all nonchalant.

"But this is," I said before he could cut me off.

"What did you hear this time, that I was out with some girl? Some girl was in my car? I was dancing with some chick at the club?"

"Wait a minute. You getting all upset and shit over a rumor. Come on man. We hear shit all the time. You gonna believe everything you hear in these motha fuckin streets? Leave that shit in the streets and keep it out of our home. Now can I finish looking at the fight please?"

"As long as it's not true then it's all good," I responded as I got up, knowing he wasn't being fully truthful.

I tried to just let it go.

"It's not true. I got too much love for you girl. Believe that mama" said Floyd as he looked over at me and smiled.

I stared at him for a minute while I got my thoughts together and then I continued talking to him about the rumor I heard.

"The rumor around town is that you got another woman pregnant!"

It was April 16, 2000, when I stopped trusting Floyd. His word became a void in my book from that day forward. I had never lied to him and I couldn't understand why he was lying to me.

"It ain't true baby. None of that shit is true," he said as he looked over at me with his puppy dog eyes.

I smiled, got up and headed to the bedroom. Before I could get there my eyes filled up with uncontrollable tears that began streaming down my face.

"You okay baby?" Floyd yelled out as I walked away.

I raised my thumb and kept walking. I was trying to keep my composure, but all I could think about was how this bastard got another woman pregnant while I was carrying his child. The fact that he would cheat on me and without protecting himself! He put our baby and me at risk, and to top it all off, he lied about it. He wasn't a real man, he could not admit his faults, apologize, and he still has the nerve to lie to my face today.

Nothing Lasts Forever

Mo' Money, Mo' Hoes

The one thing most of us women need to realize is that, for men, the mo' money they get the mo' hoes they will attract. I remember hearing people say, "you can't turn a hoe into a housewife," and "you can take a man out of the hood but you can't take the hood out the man." I know that doesn't apply to everyone, but there are a lot of people that these phrases fit. I am sure my readers will know exactly what I mean through their own experiences, or through someone else's story.

I feel that some men are better off being broke, especially when they come from nothing. Don't get me wrong, there are some broke men who find ways to attract hoes too. Of course, I wish everyone the best, but it's important to know how to act, both when you have everything and nothing at all. Be grateful if you have a damn good woman.

A hoe is just a hoe. I'm not talking about these young kids, but adults. Usually, what you see is what you get and it all comes with a price. Some hoes only want something to eat and a blunt to smoke, and there others that want a Bentley and a Hermes bag. Some hoes look for a desperate, lonely man to marry so they can be taken care of, and other hoes just want a rich baby daddy to help pay their bills and take care of the kids.

What most of us women should learn to do is listen. Truly listen and find out what the man is looking for. What do men really want from women? Do they want to be married? Do they really want a family? Do they only want sex? By listening, they will tell us everything we need to know, including what they really want. Don't get me wrong, there are some men who will lie and deceive to get you in the bed for a one-night-stand, but I want to believe that deep down, most men have good intentions.

If a man only wants sex it will most likely come up in the first conversation. Most men who are ready to settle down and have a family will mention their desires in conversation. Don't be afraid to ask questions when you first meet someone; you have nothing to lose. Ask about his upbringing. Did both parents raise him? Did his parents have the same values? Was he raised in different households? Was there domestic violence in his home? Don't be ashamed to ask about his debts and credit. Where does he see himself in five, ten, or fifteen years? Does he want to get married? Are kids in his future? You should want to know if his future plans have room for you. I'm not a therapist, but I'm speaking from my own experiences and mistakes. I didn't grow up knowing my father, so I didn't have a male role model around to teach me about boys and men. I blame this for the mistakes I've made when it comes to choosing men.

When I listen to old stories of hard-working men, who used to get up early in the morning to go to work to support his family, come home, spend quality time with his wife and kids, I think to myself, Wow! Where are those men today? My generation doesn't breed that type of man anymore. In the twenty-first century, the few guys I know sit around playing video games all day and night. I rarely see those same values in men today: good work ethic, family oriented, and willing to sacrifice. The woman took care of the home, made sure the house was clean, food was prepared, the kids were in order, and their home was their sanctuary.

We are in a lost generation. Not many people want to do the right thing to get ahead, they find a way to take a shortcut instead. We have women having sex in exchange for money and gifts. Young girls stand on street corners selling their precious bodies. Why do we, as women, think so little of ourselves? So many of us have become lazy and dependent on people or ways of life. Receiving income through the county and child support only lasts until your child turns 18 years old. I don't want to put anyone down, but we need to do better and yes, I said we, because I am a part of this stigma too. Looking back, I was unknowingly Floyd's private hoe; I was not good enough to become Mrs. Mayweather and yet I stayed. He didn't want me to mess with any other man but yet he didn't want to be loyal or faithful to me either. This is a continuous cycle that happens to so many women, and we all must open our eyes and learn to expect more from our relationships.

Toxic Masculinity

Most men take their masculinity too far. The problem I had with Floyd was that he refused to listen to me, as if what I had to say was unimportant. He felt that since he was earning millions of dollars com[pared to my nickels and dimes, that I should become his follower— that he was the leader. Everything became all about him; his wants, his needs. He was the tough one in the relationship, while I was the sensitive one. There was no me in the relationship, only he, himself, and him. Floyd hid his emotions. Whenever I expressed what was on my mind, I became more and more vulnerable.

I would sit and wait up for him to come home, and he would rarely show up. When he felt like having sex, I was sexually available to him. Knowing he was with some other woman, having it his way and cheating without any regard to my feeling, he still would come and be with me as if he had done nothing wrong. Floyd was a perpetrator and master manipulator and I became his victim over and over again. It's sad that men don't see women as their equals. Some of them treat us like a new car: They drive us for a while, break us in, and later park us in the garage where we sit, rarely used.

How do you turn a man back on after he's been turned off? Is it even possible to bring back any good once it's gone? Why as women do we keep trying once all hope is lost? For almost 20 years I tried to keep him interested in me and our family, until I realized it was my dream not his, and that I was only hurting myself.

If you come across a man who has any of the traits I just described, run in the other direction. It's toxic behavior and isn't good for anyone. If you hang around long enough, it can rub off on you, causing you to act the same way. I thank God for protecting me from becoming toxic and helping me to recognize toxic behavior. In all of my future relationships, I will have the knowledge to identify toxic behavior and to get out before things get out of control.

There were a few times when I picked fights with Floyd. I saw myself becoming more like him and less like myself. Toxic people can bring out the worst in you if you let them. It's important to be mindful of your surroundings and pay attention to the people in your life. Watch for warning signs and don't be afraid to address them or to leave the situation if you have to. If you're able to leave a problem or bad situation early, it makes things so much better for all parties involved, especially when there are kids. Toxic behavior can affect and entire family, and that can be a very dangerous situation.

A Quick Flashback

September 2010, a very humiliating and painful public beat-down took place. I wasn't the only person who was receiving beat-downs. In 2012, Floyd put hands on another woman by the name of Miss Jackson, twisting her arm and choking her. I also heard that he pulled a gun on her and threatened to shoot off her toes. And the stories of abuse don't stop. I don't know why I ever thought he could change. He has done so much and it never gets better because he never serves any real time. It just shows that money is power.

Now Floyd is facing major lawsuits. After all he has put me through, you'd think he would have learned a lesson but apparently not. If he kept his damn hands to himself outside the ring, he wouldn't be in the mess he's in today. Enough of everybody else's drama. Back to my reality.

Money And Ignorance Equal Failure

The Beat-down Continues

September 9, 2010

Excruciating, searing pain blasted through my head. A blinding flash of light penetrated my brain as I tried to open my eyes. I thought my head was exploding, and I heard myself scream; my body struggled out of a foggy sleep. I felt myself falling… no, I was being pulled off the sofa. Was this a terrible nightmare?

When I hit the floor, it jolted me into awareness of what was happening, and I looked up as I tried to gain some traction with my feet to fight off this nightmare. But it was no nightmare—it was a real predator. I was not surprised when I saw it was Floyd, nor when I realized he was trying to hurt me that night. It had happened before, but this time, it felt as though it would be my last day on earth. As I gained enough energy all I could do was scream "FLOYD NOOOOO!"

Floyd had been calling me all night, sending text messages with photographs of him with the kids. My mind was reeling with questions. How had he gotten into the house? Prior to this evening, I had issued a restraining order! On this particular evening, Floyd didn't give a damn whether the kids were in the house or not. When he started to walk toward me, the first thing that came to mind was my cell phone, so I reached for my purse. With all of the yelling and screaming, I was nervous, so I couldn't find it.

"You motha fuckin' bitch," Floyd screamed, looking down at me. "Are you fuckin' around on me, bitch, with that punk-ass nigga? I'll kill you and that bitch-ass nigga."

He snatched me by my hair, holding me up like a puppet on a string hanging from the ceiling. It felt like my scalp was ripping off. He was so strong. At any given moment, he could break my neck in two and leave me on the floor to die.

"Stop, stop, stop! You're hurting me Floyd, please stop! Let go! Please! I'm begging you, Floyd. It's not what you think—"

"I been callin' your tramp ass all night. Were you fuckin' him? Too busy to answer your phone?" he looked at me, wild eyed. He leaned over, and in a cruel tone, he hissed into my ear, "I'll kill you and my kids and go to prison for life before I let any other man come into my house, where I'm paying the bills, fuck my woman, eat my food, and play daddy to my sons. And if you don't believe me…try me."

He threw me across the coffee table, and it tipped over as I tried to kick him. The table was extremely heavy; it fell on my torso, and I cracked my head as it toppled over on me. I felt another bash to my head. That bash was his fist. Now I was dizzy, and I started to feel sick to my stomach. All I could think about were my kids. I struggled to stay conscious. I shook my head and tried to stand, but I fell to the floor.

He lunged at me again. This time his fists were clenched. I knew if he hit me again, I'd be out. I dodged the blow with my hands, crawling toward the front door. My mind was still racing as I tried to survive his rage. I had no weapon with which to fight him off. Mind you, his hands were registered weapons. I could have threatened him, but how do you threaten someone who is afraid of nothing and no one? For a second, I felt as though my life was over at the age of thirty. "If I call the police, they are going to take you to jail for hitting me and threatening to kill me and the kids. You have a restraining order, and I can make sure you never see me or your kids again!" I screamed as he came at me again. "You're a pimp just like your father, and you act just like him. You have more women than you can count. I'm tired, Floyd; I can't do it anymore. I can't live with the lies and the broken promises—it's destroying everything we've worked for. How do you say you love me and then try to kill me? You're like poison, Floyd."

He took a few steps back and fell to the floor. He stared at me for a few minutes before saying anything.

"You know none of those bitches mean anything to me. You're mine, Josie, and that will never change." His eyes were blazing as he spoke. "You and the kids belong to me." Floyd was speaking, but he had so much anger, he sounded as though he were some sort of animal.

I spotted my cell phone on the floor near my purse. I grabbed it and dialed 9-1-1 and waited for a few seconds. I tried to speak into the phone: "Please, send someone; I'm bleeding. Floyd Mayweather just beat the shit out of me. I'm his ex-girlfriend, Josie Harris. He threatened to kill me and the kids."

"Calm down, ma'am. Can I have the address you're calling from?" said the operator.

"Bitch!" he shouted out as he paced the room.

My sons, Koraun and Zion along with my daughter Jirah, were standing at the stairs, staring at the blood running down my face. Jirah started to cry and yell, "Mama! Mama!"

I tried to gather my thoughts and remain calm. "It's okay, babies," I said, looking at them, shaking and crying. I found the strength to lift myself up off the floor, and I walked over and hugged them. My whole body was pounding with pain while the blood trailed behind me.

The operator on the other end of the phone was trying to calm me down.

"I'm going to need the address in order to send someone out."

My oldest son, Koraun, took the phone from my hand and gave the operator the address.

"We are sending someone right now. Is he still in the house? Does he have a weapon? Where are the children?" she asked.

Koraun handed the phone to me.

"Hello," I said as I tried to calm myself.

"Where are the children?"

"They're here in my arms."

"Is Mr. Mayweather still in the house?"

"He's still in the house."

I looked over at Floyd. He looked back at me in anger and then, he started to pace back and forth. He tried to reach for my cell phone.

I yelled, "He's trying to take the phone!"

"I'm right here," the operator said comfortingly.

I looked at Floyd. He still looked angry, and he was pacing. He tried to reach for my cell phone again. Floyd took the phone from my hand, threw it on the floor, and stomped on it.

"Floyd, the police are on their way," I said, thinking it would bring him to his senses. I looked over at the doorway of the living room, and the kids were watching us; they were scared and crying.

"Mommy, Daddy, please don't fight," said my daughter, Jirah, as the tears ran down her face.

Koraun and Zion were looking around, wide eyed, waiting for their father's next move. Floyd wouldn't look at them.

Jirah kept crying, "I'm scared, Mommy."

"Floyd, if you touch them, I swear I'll kill you, so help me God."

I felt my heart turn to stone at that moment, and I knew I would do anything I could to protect my children.

"Hello, hello. Are you still there?" the operator asked.

"He just ran out of the house. He's driving a white Bentley sedan."

"Are you able to get the license plate number?"

"The license plate number is TS57B9P. He's heading toward Henderson Avenue and Queen Street," I answered.

A police car arrived at my home. I ran to the front door to let them in.

"May I get your first and last name?" one officer asked me.

"My name is Josie Harris."

The second police officer walked toward me and asked, "Would you like for us to call an ambulance and have you checked out?"

"No sir. I'll be alright," I answered.

"Are you sure you don't want us to call an ambulance? You're really bleeding a lot."

"No, please. It will just scare the kids."

"We understand Ma'am, but due to your injuries and all the blood we need to call to have them at least take a look. Did the kids see him hit you?"

"I'm not sure. I don't know what they saw."

A third police officer arrived, and he went into the bedroom to speak with the boys.

"I understand that your son Koraun let Mr. Mayweather in through the back-bedroom door. Does Mr. Mayweather know he has a restraining order?"

The police officers looked at me.

"Yes, he does."

"Do you want to press charges?" the other police officer asked.

"Yes, I do. He threatened to kill both me and my kids."

One of the police officers took a domestic abuse report. A few minutes later an ambulance pulled up. They placed me on a stretcher and took me to the ER. I promised myself that that would be the last beat-down I would ever take from Floyd.

How Did I Get Here?

The clock on the nightstand read: 3:41 AM. I suddenly woke from a deep sleep. I sat up in my bed and realized I had been sweating. Barely able to breath, I reached over and turned on the lamp. I stared outside my window and that's when it hit me. I asked myself out loud, "Why did I stay so long in such an abusive and toxic relationship?"

The first time he started doing things to me I began to have nightmares. When the small incidents turned to beatings, I developed insomnia. Years of abuse messed me up and changed my personality, not for the better. I lost my identity. I had to maintain false realities in order to deal with everyday issues. Going along with the bullshit became a normal lifestyle for me without me even realizing it.

Love is a powerful thing, especially when you're young and don't know the true meaning or value of love. As a kid, you don't know how to choose love, receive love, or how to love at all. Every time I thought about how Floyd treated me, I would drink the pain away. For every hit I took, I ate. "How did I get here?" I asked myself over and over, never able to come up with an answer that made sense.

Was I just a weak, naïve woman who thought she was strong? Did the player somehow play me? Was I trying to turn a bad man into a good man? I still ask myself these same questions while I thirst for Floyd's love and affection. My love for him never stopped but his love for me ended a long time ago, if he ever loved me at all. I don't understand how a man can tell you, "You're the only one I love," and turn around and pick up some hood rat bitch, take her out for dinner, fuck her, spend the night at a five-star hotel, take the bitch shopping the next morning, and then come home later, kiss me on the cheek and say, "I love you. What's for dinner babe?" My conscience would never allow me to do anything as fucked up as that to anyone.

Many people may think I'm angry because I had a man—or should I say a boy—who cheated. I'm not angry. Now when I was young and stupid, I did young and stupid things like many of us. As I matured, I realized that there were thirsty women and tramps out there that wanted what I had: The lifestyle, the car I drove, the shoes I wore, and the man I slept with. I understand the game, even if I don't agree with it, and for the rest of my life I will continue to ask myself: "How did I get here?"

The Cycle Of Domestic Violence

The Final Kick

Here we go again! Just when I thought the last beat-down was the final beat-down, I gave in to his bullshit again. I gave him another chance to do right by me and our children. Things seemed to be going fine. We did things like a normal family. The arguments had stopped and he never raised his hand at me. It was good. If I had to guess how many times Floyd physically abused me, I would have to say at least a dozen times throughout our entire relationship.

I know this may seem like I'm making excuses for him, but I always felt that maybe he was under too much stress from his career. I didn't take the abuse as serious as I should have. I kept finding excuses for him. I sat back and realized that in most families, especially broken families, no one ever teaches you how you should be treated, or how to carry yourself as a young woman. For these people, life is almost always self-taught, meaning that it is only through mistakes and trial and error that we discover what is acceptable and what is not.

I can recall moments when I wouldn't leave the house because I didn't want anyone to see my black eyes or busted lips. I refused to let my family visit me because I was embarrassed, confused, scared, ashamed, and didn't want to be asked a thousand questions. Most people don't understand that sometimes the best support you can give a victim of domestic violence are words of comfort.

I recall one unforgettable moment when Floyd decided to kick me directly in the vagina, causing me to bleed for three weeks. I the pain like it was yesterday; the first night was the worst. I felt as though I was giving birth to triplets. I didn't realize how bad it was until I ran into the bathroom, removed my panties, and blood was running down both my legs onto the floor. Floyd stood at the bathroom door knocking like he was the FBI. "Open the door bitch before I break this motha fucka down!" he yelled. At that very moment the only thing on my mind was stopping the bleeding and hoping this wasn't my last day on earth. I couldn't call 9-1-1 because I had left my cell phone on the sofa, where I was sitting when Floyd started to act like a madman. After a while of cleaning myself up and trying to distract myself from the pain, it appeared that Floyd had left.

When I thought he was gone, I finally got myself together and slowly came out of the bathroom. I had prepared myself to be thrown, punched, or kicked all over again, but to my surprise, he didn't do that at all. In fact, he was still sitting there on the sofa watching Sport Center like the horrible event had just taken place did not happen at all. I sat across from him wrapped in a bath towel and stared, trying to understand how he could show no emotion. Did he have any idea the pain that he had just caused? Did he simply not care? I was too angry and overwhelmed with pain to cry or to say anything. Later that night I made my way into the bedroom and fell asleep.

In the wee hours of the morning, while I was sound asleep, I felt Floyd get in the bed. I slowly opened my eyes, trying to figure out his intentions. Then it happened. He snatched the towel from around my body, turned me over, spread my legs while I was still bleeding, and started to have his way with me. He fucked me like I was a dog.

There was no "I'm sorry" or "Forgive me." He just laid on top of me sweating and panting until he reached his unwelcome climax. When he was done, he laid there with such a satisfied look on his face, with absolutely no remorse for his actions. I climbed out of the blood-stained bed and made my way back to the bathroom. I could feel the blood dripping down my legs with every step. I turned on the bath water and I lay there, mind racing. Then there was a knock on the door. I jumped in fear. It was Floyd.

"I'm gone. Holla at you later, I got some business to handle."

I didn't say a word but I heard the door close. Not only did I choose to stay in the house after he inflicted all this pain, I made it worse by refusing to call 9-1-1 for help. I allowed him to have sex with me while I bled. The pain I endured was unbearable. All I could do was ask myself why? Why did I keep taking this kind of punishment? What did I do to deserve this? Is this really love? Is love supposed to hurt this bad? Will it ever get better? Please God show me the light and give me the strength to walk away for good.

I lived with a man who said he loved me but beat the shit out of me. One morning, Floyd beat me so bad while the kids were at school that when I went to the bathroom to wipe the blood from my mouth, I realized I had had a bowel movement. I can only guess that I was so numb from the pain of his blows, that I didn't realize what had happened. I've heard the term "I will

beat the shit out of you," but I never knew that it was actually possible until it happened to me. That was the final kick!

Good Girls Finish Last

I considered myself a good woman to Floyd. I cooked, I cleaned, I washed clothes, and gave him three beautiful children. I loved him, trusted him, and I made him my king. These were things I thought a good woman did. But I see now that good women finish last and the no-good bitches finish first.

It isn't fair: Good women tend to be treated like shit. We're taken advantage of and our hard work is just time wasted. Sometimes I wonder if being a good woman is worth it, but becoming someone I'm not would be much harder. I recall a conversation I had with a much older woman. I explained my situation to her and what she said to me I'll never forget: "Baby, don't change for anyone. Be true to who you are. If you change, you're no different than the others. One day God will send you a good man that you are meant to be with. A man who finds a wife finds a good thing, a favor from the Lord." That's when it hit me. I realized that day that I was too damn good for Floyd and that he would never appreciate me.

I also came to realize that it's not all Floyd's fault, it's mine too. I allowed him to use me, disrespect me, call me out of my name, slap me, beat me, kick me, bring STDs into our relationship, and worst of all, have a child with another woman. I enabled him by going back to him. Floyd only did what I allowed him to do. Sometimes a good woman falls in love with a bad man, and she forgets how good she is until someone reminds her. I forgot who I was because I got caught up in his life. I forgot I even had a life that was worth living.

113

Signs Of Depression

"Hurry up kids, mommy does not want you to be late for school!" As I gathered the kids and got them into the car safely, I headed to drop them off at school. "You guys have a great day," I said as they made their way out of the car. I headed back to the house to relax a little before beginning my day; I kicked my shoes off, removed my clothes, and fell into the sofa as I took a deep breath. "It's good to be back home," I said to myself, reaching for the remote so I could catch up on the news. After a few minutes of listening to who had been shot, breaking news comes across the TV: It's another high-speed chase, someone stole a car from someone now he's on the run. I decided to get up to pour myself a glass of wine to unwind. Maybe it was too early to be drinking but if you had walked a mile in my shoes, and suffered from the things I had, you too would have a drink.

I started to notice that I would feel sad and have wandering thoughts when the kids weren't around. My mind started to go back to the time when Floyd and I were a happy, or at least so I thought. Two young kids having fun, hanging out at the movies eating popcorn, and being in love. But then I began thinking about the other women who came into the picture when I believed it was just Floyd and me against the world. I'd go back to the different times he cheated on me, the fights I had with women he screwed around with, and the hardest one of all: accepting that he got another women pregnant just six months after I found out I was pregnant with our first son. I gave him so much time and energy I can never get back. It was me who played the fool and let him run over me time and time again. I thought staying and being a great mom, supporter, and lover

114

despite everything, would show him one day that I was the one.

The more I gave the more he took advantage of me, and sadly, I never could see it for what it really was. This is where I believe my depression came from; all the hurt and pain for so many years, but also believing in something that will never come to be. I didn't realize that all of the things I endured in my past would one day overwhelm me, and affect my life in such a negative way. I did eventually to therapy, and was diagnosed with depression, anxiety, and PTSD. In my younger years, I would never have sought therapy, but today I am so grateful for my decision to finally seek help. Yet I still deal with the pain, and even today, I'm an unhappy 30-year-old woman. I have no one to blame but myself, because I allowed Floyd to take my heart and break it into a thousand pieces. He moved on with his life, while I hung on, still wishing what we used to have would return one day; still being naïve enough to go running back like nothing ever happened.

Where did my wine go? Let me pour myself another glass and take my depression and anxiety meds. I toast to being free from bullshit. As much as I would like to say the meds are working and I'm getting better, I don't always feel that way. I always question my value: Am I really a great mom, especially now that I have to take these drugs? Am I a good person? What is my purpose here on earth? Am I drinking too much? Why does food have to be so good and makes me feel good? These are some questions I ask myself every day. I drink because it makes me relax and makes me happy temporarily. I eat because it gives me comfort, and I take these meds because I was told it would make me feel better. I am trying. I put on a pair of jeans the other morning and they didn't fit me anymore. I also believe my weight gain has added to my depression, anxiety, and lack of confidence. Of course, I never thought I would stay the same weight forever, but I didn't expect to gain this much weight in my thirties. My doctor mentioned that one of the side effects of my meds could be weight gain or increased eating habits. When Floyd started dating Miss Jackson, I felt a little jealous; it bothered me because I felt like he was trading me in for a newer version of my old self. I knew this time we were officially done forever.

After three children and being there damn near since the beginning, always supporting him through it all, he made me feel like it was all for nothing. I could never understand why men, especially black men, could be with a such good woman, but once he makes it and becomes "someone," he leaves her or pushes her to the curb. A new woman just walks in and enjoys the fruit of your labor and all you invested in. The times we had to put nickels and dimes together to get something to eat, the times we could barely pay our bills—those seem like the happiest times looking back, because we knew we had each other. It's thoughts like these that cause me to want a drink and eat.

I cannot just sit and dwell on the negative when I have done things. Something big for me started back in 2001 when I started to write my tell-all book. Writing my story was a way to vent and let it all out. I also started to prepare myself to be a Reality Star on my own reality TV show. I wanted to create a diaper bag for mother's with newborn children—a long-time dream of mine. But the past few years I lost my motivation to get myself going.

I recall the times when I would stay up all night long working on a project and wake up early in the morning to work some more. I was this creative soul who wanted to do so much before I left this earth. I wanted to leave a legacy for my children and their children and so on. As I drink the last drop of wine from my glass, I look over at the clock I realize I still have four hours and thirty-seven minutes before I have to pick up the kids from school. What am I going to do? Sit in this damn house all alone trying to motivate myself. But I end up with negative thoughts that bring such unhappiness. They say, "The past is the past and what's in the past needs to stay in the past." Well! Easier said than done. The past is all I have to think about because I don't know who I am and I don't know what my future holds.

A woman can get so lost into a man that she cannot remember who she is. Sometimes I wonder if I had a man—I'm talking about a real man who would love me and take me in his arms and never let me go–would I be happy? I often wonder if there is anyone else out there besides Floyd that I could love.

I know what I need to do: I need to get up, put on my workout clothes, go to the gym, and work out for an hour to release some stress and frustration before picking the kids up. I get up, make my way to the shower, get dressed, sit down on the edge of the bed to put on my tennis shoes and then it happens. I lay back to relax for a minute or two and fall asleep. When I wake its time to pick up the kids. Another day, no gym, no writing, nothing accomplished, and all this wishful thinking. Another day, and I've allowed this depression, anxiety, and PTSD to have its way with me for seven hours. At least when my children jump in the car, these things seem to drift away. All I can do is hope and pray that tomorrow is a better day.

My Broken Heart

As I sit here in my bathtub with a glass of chilled white wine, I think back on my life and the drama I endured and it makes my heart ache. I still have a broken heart. How did I let Floyd do this? Was it because I was so in love? Was it because of his charm? Or was it because I was just too damn blind to recognize the signs? When your heart has been broken into a thousand pieces, healing is like putting together a thousand piece puzzle—it's challenging, and it can take a very long time, if it ever happens at all.

My heart will never heal from all the hurt and pain that man put me through, yet I still don't think I'll ever love another man like I loved him. They say if you keep your heart open, someone will find their way in; I don't believe that anymore. Even if my heart was open, my mind is closed to the mere idea of love. It would be so hard to trust again after my spirit has been broken by the men in my life.

It's crazy to think that my life has come to an end, while his is beginning. I remember one day in church the minister said, "God so loved the world…" I used to hope and pray that Floyd would love me like God loves Us. Unconditional love inspires you; it understands your mistakes and all your imperfections. I feel like that type of love doesn't exist today. People are selfish, mean, and social only adds fuel to the fire.

I ask myself every single day: "How can I recover from a broken heart? Can it be mended?" I find myself eating and drinking like there's no tomorrow. I wake up with intentions of going to the gym, but many days I find myself having trouble getting out of bed because I'm so depressed. Floyd has put me through hell and back and I have a t-shirt to prove it. I don't wish anything bad on him but I truly believe that "Every dog has its day and what goes up must come down." We should treat others with kindness and love your brothers and sisters as you love yourself. For all the women out there that are suffering from a broken heart, my advice is to find a way to heal your heart. It will take work, but it's never too late to start the healing process. I wish I had started sooner.

Woman In The Mirror

As I stand in the mirror brushing my teeth, I pause for a moment, remove my toothbrush, rinse my mouth out and I stand there looking at myself. In that moment I see sixteen-year-old me. The young girl that went through things that most teenage girls have never experienced. If my father had stayed in my life would things be different? Maybe or maybe not. As much as I'd like to think that having both of my parents around would have changed the outcome of my life, I can't assume. Did living in poverty, watching my mom work two jobs just to get by, and being a minority affect I grew into a woman? Maybe or maybe not.

I wish adult Josie could speak to young Josie. What would I need to say to her? I would tell her to go to college, get a job, travel, and enjoy life before finding a husband and having children and living happily ever after. I tell her not to date a boy who had a dream of becoming a champion boxer. I would tell her not to have three children with him, not to stay in the relationship despite his abuse and disrespect. I would tell her to run Josie, run! No one knows the future but God. Did I miss His signs because I was young and not listening? People warned me to leave Floyd but I stayed. I would tell young Josie to listen to that advice, to leave at the

119

first sign of trouble. Why didn't I leave? The answer always comes back the same: because of love, and my hope that I could have a happy family with the man I was so in love with. Watch out for the signs of a domestic abuser. He/she will attempt to use reverse psychology, over-apologizing for their actions and sometimes even crying, by playing the victim. I believe I stayed because I didn't know what the future held. I didn't know if I would have the support I needed. I still wanted my children to have both parents in the same home. I wasn't sure if I would be accepted or loved by someone else because I had three kids and was no longer the sweet, innocent girl I used to be; I felt like damaged goods. If I could, I would tell my younger self to be strong and never to believe that anything was her fault. Some may believe I stayed because of the fame and fortune, the Bentley and diamonds. It was nice sometimes, can destroy relationships.

I stayed in an abusive relationships that was mentally and emotionally damaging to my well-being now. My mind said leave but my heart said stay; how could I choose? My mind played tricks on me for many years: believing not seeing, seeing not believing. Thinking I could play superwoman and put everything back to the way it was. Domestic violence became my new normal. Where did I go wrong? At what point did I get lost, unable to find my way back? While waiting and hoping he would change, I should have made that change for myself. I've come to realize that there are millions of domestic violence victims in the world and about 90% are living in fear. They learn to accept their new "normal" because of love, money, material things, stability, or lust. No one really knows what it's like to be a victim of abuse until they've been one themselves.

Sometimes it takes time to realize when enough is enough, and sometimes victims don't ever get the time. Lots of domestic violence victims never get the chance to experience freedom and true happiness. I did and I hope others can too. If I could say one very important thing to young girls it's this: Never stay silent if you're being abused—it's okay to walk away and tell someone you love.

Tears roll down my face as I stare in the mirror, but they're tears of joy too because I overcame my hardships and it's now my turn to help others and to show them they are not alone. I wipe my face, pick up my toothbrush, and finish brushing my teeth. I can carry on knowing I have my freedom, my children, and that I will learn true happiness.

A Mother's Love

Being a mother has brought so much joy into my life. My children are my sunshine, my light, the air I breathe, my strength, my everything. I don't know where I would be if I didn't have them to fall back. They run into my bedroom and jump on my bed and hug me with all their might when I'm at my lowest. They make me feel loved and deep in my heart I know it's unconditional. A mother's love can never be replaced. There's something about being a mom that there are not enough words to explain. Having someone that depends on you and looks to you for guidance and direction. Being a mom means wearing many hats. Motherhood is more than giving birth. It's changing diapers, feeding, and making your children feel safe. Teaching them how to walk, talk, read, write, and potty-training. A mother's job is 24/7, 365 days a year. I know having children gave me something to live for other than myself.

My hope is that my children recognize how much I love them; that I do my best to give them the love they deserve and more. I wish they hadn't witnessed the things that went down between Floyd and me. I never want my children to dislike their father, but my wish is that my sons grow up knowing that it's never okay to hit, slap, kick, beat, or use force on a woman. A woman isn't a punching bag, nor is she a man's property. A woman is so many beautiful things that deserves to be respected and cherished. Kudos to the mothers who put their children first, who love them relentlessly. Motherhood is truly the best gift from God.

Josie's Favorite Bible Verse

"So when they continued asking him, he lifted himself up, and said unto them, he that is without sin among you, let him first cast a stone at her."

John 8: verse 7

The King James Version

Love Can Break You, But Common Sense Can Strengthen You

The Final TKO

Floyd Mayweather Wins Again

Another TKO goes to the best pound-for-pound fighter, Floyd Mayweather Jr. When Josie Harris passed away on March 09, 2020, Floyd no longer had the responsibility of paying child support, supporting Josie's lifestyle, paying legal fees to defend himself against domestic violence charges, or standing in court against the $20,000,000 defamation lawsuit filed against him after Floyd allegedly lied during an interview with Katie Couric in April 2015, saying that Josie was a drug abuser. The defamation case was scheduled to go to trial on December 7, 2020.

The 20 years of drama between Josie and Floyd are officially over. Floyd will never have to wonder if his ex is seeing someone else. He no longer has to worry about the possibility of going to prison for domestic violence against Josie. I'm sure Mr. Mayweather knew Josie was no match for him throughout their 20 years in battle. Prior to Josie Harris' death, Floyd's fight record was 50 wins with no losses. His new record is 51 wins and…

A Broken Legal System

When did a cell phone worth a few hundred bucks become more valuable than a human being's life? Mayweather was charged on two counts for beating Josie in 2010. The first count was Grand Larceny for damaging Josie's cell phone, which was a FELONY but count two for battery was a MISDEMEANOR.

There's truly something wrong with our legal system. A woman's ex-boyfriend can beat her half to death and receive no jail time, nor a fine. Mayweather did not serve time for the real crime that was committed but served a small amount of time for damaging her cell phone. Is a material thing really worth more than a life?

Josie Harris Gone Too Soon

On March 9, 2020, deputies with the Santa Clarita Valley Sheriff Station were called for medical rescue in Valencia at 9:42PM. They found an unresponsive woman in a car, parked in what investigators believe was her driveway. Officials arrived and she was pronounced dead at the scene. Later it was confirmed to be Josie Harris, a 40-year-old female. The cause of Josie's death is still unknown.

Josie's death was unexpected and she will be missed by those who loved and cared for her. Her twelve rounds came to an end that day, and she was finally able to hang up her gloves. Even though it appears that Josie lost like anyone.

The Biggest Loss and Win

Josie Harris' lost was bigger than anyone could imagine. She'll never see her only daughter attend her high school prom, graduate, go to college, attend her wedding, or have the opportunity to become a grandmother. She will never see the men her two sons will become. Her death has certainly disrupted her children's foundation, their sense of security and safety. One can only hope that her children will be surrounded by love and support, and the terrible things they witnessed over the years will be an example of what wrong for them.

Josie Harris' Hope

Josie's hope is that all victims of domestic violence will one day live without fear, pain, and most importantly, that they know they are not alone. Her spirit can now rest knowing that her story has been told. She wanted more than anything to share her story, in hopes of educating young men and women on an issues that doesn't get the attention it should. Allow your voices to be heard; continue to protest and fight to protect victims of domestic violence. The fight must continue. A silent voice can be our worst enemy.

CPSIA information can be obtained
at www.ICGtesting.com
Printed in the USA
LVHW080435230720
661002LV00028B/674